BROKEN BEYOND: HEALING FROM TERRAIN OF LOVE

SANKET CHAUDHARY

To those who inspired me and will not read it

Contents

Contents

Part 1

Foreword

Heartbreak is a universal experience that can be one of the most difficult challenges we face in life. It can leave us feeling lost, alone, and overwhelmed with emotions that seem impossible to navigate. It is during these moments that we need guidance and support to help us heal and move forward.

The book you hold in your hands, "Broken Beyond," is a comprehensive guide to overcoming the pain of heartbreak and finding a way to a happier, healthier life. The author, a first-time writer, has poured their heart and soul into this book to offer practical advice and strategies for anyone who has experienced the pain of a broken heart.

Through their own personal experiences and research, the author has crafted a powerful tool for those who are seeking to heal and grow. This book offers a roadmap to the healing process and provides valuable insights into the psychological, physical, and emotional impact of heartbreak. It is a guide that offers hope, encouragement, and a path forward.

As you read this book, you will find practical exercises, tips, and tools that will help you navigate the difficult terrain of heartbreak. The author has written this book with empathy, compassion, and a deep understanding of the pain that comes with heartbreak. They have included their own stories and experiences to create a relatable and heartfelt guide.

Acknowledgements

I am deeply grateful to everyone who has supported me in writing this book on healing from heartbreak. First and foremost, I would like to thank my dear friends Shrikar Nakhye, Aditya Khare, Manay Chawra,Yugal Chauhan and many others for their unwavering encouragement and support throughout this journey. Your friendship means the world to me. Your unwavering support and encouragement have been instrumental in helping me complete this project.

I would also like to express my gratitude to my loving family, especially my dad, for always believing in me and pushing me to pursue my dreams and providing me with a solid foundation to build upon. Your love and support have been my rock during difficult times. Your love and guidance have been invaluable.

To my ex-partner Ruchika Gaidhani and Tejal Chaudhary thank you for being a part of my life and for teaching me valuable lessons about love, loss and Myself. While our relationships may not have lasted, the lessons learned have been invaluable in shaping who I am today. I wish you both happiness and fulfilment in your own journeys.

Finally, I would like to acknowledge the many authors who have written on similar topics and whose work has inspired and informed my own. Your research and insights have provided me with a deeper understanding of the complex nature of heartbreak and have inspired me to continue exploring this important topic. Your contributions to the field of personal growth and healing are invaluable.

Thank you all for your love, support, and inspiration. This book would not have been possible without you.

Preface

Heartbreak is a universal experience that touches us all at some point in our lives. It is a painful and challenging process that can leave us feeling lost, alone, and uncertain about the future. However, it is also a transformative experience that can lead to growth, healing, and a renewed sense of purpose and meaning.

The purpose of this book is to provide a roadmap for navigating the healing journey from heartbreak. Throughout the book, you will find a range of topics and perspectives, from understanding the science of heartbreak to practical strategies for self-care and healing.

Our hope is that this book will serve as a guide and source of inspiration for anyone who is going through heartbreak. We believe that by embracing the pain, exploring our emotions, and taking intentional steps towards healing, we can emerge from heartbreak with newfound strength, resilience, and clarity about our values and goals.

We are grateful to our contributors and experts who have shared their wisdom and experiences, and to our readers who are embarking on the journey of healing from heartbreak. We hope that this book will be a valuable resource for you on your journey towards healing and transformation.

Prologue

Love is a beautiful feeling that can make our lives vibrant and meaningful. But when that love ends, it can leave behind a trail of pain and heartbreak that can be difficult to cope with. As someone who has been through the heartbreak of a failed relationship, I know first-hand how difficult it can be to pick up the pieces and move forward.

But as time went on, I began to learn about the many ways in which we can heal from heartbreak. From the power of music and exercise to the importance of social support, I discovered that there are many tools and techniques that we can use to navigate the difficult terrain of heartbreak.

In this book, I hope to share with you what I have learned about healing from heartbreak. Whether you are going through a breakup right now or simply looking to build your resilience for the future, I believe that the insights and strategies in this book can help you find your way through the pain and emerge stronger and more resilient than ever before. So let's begin our journey towards healing together.

About The Author

Sanket chaudhary is a first-time author who has poured his heart and soul into his debut book, "Broken Beyond: healing from terrain of love". He has dedicated himself to researching and compiling the most effective strategies for healing and moving on from heartbreak. He hopes that his book will provide comfort, guidance, and healing to those who need it most.

Note From Author

Dear Reader,

I am thrilled to share with you my book on healing from heartbreak. In this book, I delve into the emotional and psychological challenges of ending a relationship and offer practical advice for moving forward and finding happiness again.

Heartbreak is a universal experience that can leave us feeling lost, confused, and overwhelmed. But I believe that with the right tools and support, we can heal and grow from these experiences, and even come out stronger and more resilient on the other side.

Throughout the book, I explore important topics such as the difference between needs and neediness, coping mechanisms for men and women, the role of self-care and self-compassion, and the power of forgiveness and gratitude.

I draw on my own personal experiences as well as my professional expertise as a therapist to provide insights and guidance for anyone going through a difficult breakup. My hope is that this book will be a source of comfort, support, and inspiration for anyone on the path to healing and wholeness.

Thank you for embarking on this journey with me.

Warmly,

Sanket Chaudhary

CHAPTER ONE

INTRODUCTION

"Dennis Quaid once said, "When you break up, your whole identity is shattered. It's like a death." A breakup is something you thought would never happen. Someone that has been a permanent fixture in your life is gone and it's tearing your heart to pieces."

The pain of a broken heart can be all-consuming and can feel like an overwhelming emotional burden that is difficult to overcome. It can leave one feeling empty, lost, and alone. It is important to recognize that this pain is normal and a natural part of the healing process. It is okay to take time to grieve and feel the emotions associated with heartbreak. However, it is equally important to take steps to heal and move forward.

It is important to acknowledge that healing is not a linear process and that there will be good days and bad days. There may be moments when the pain feels unbearable, but with time and effort, it will become more manageable. Taking care of oneself is critical during this time. Engaging in self-care activities such as exercise, meditation, and spending time with loved ones can help to alleviate the pain.

One of the keys to healing a broken heart is to practice self-compassion. Recognize that it is okay to make mistakes and not have all the answers. Be gentle with yourself and acknowledge that healing takes time. It is also important to avoid self-blame or blame towards others. Instead, focus on understanding the situation and moving forward with forgiveness and compassion.

Another helpful approach is to seek support from a therapist or a trusted friend or family member. Talking about one's feelings can help to process the pain and gain a new perspective on the situation. It is important to remember that seeking help is a sign of strength, not weakness.

Ultimately, healing a broken heart is a process that requires patience, self-compassion, and a willingness to let go of the past. With time, one can learn to love again and find joy in life.

CHAPTER TWO

NAVIGATING THE BREAKUP PROCESS: A GUIDE TO ENDING A ROMANTIC RELATIONSHIP

"The pain of parting is nothing to the joy of meeting again.- Charles Dickens"

Breaking up with a significant other can be a difficult task that no one enjoys, but it is an inevitable part of many romantic relationships. While it may seem daunting, many academic and professional studies can guide you through the breakup process. This chapter will provide you with the tools you need to navigate the breakup process, from deciding to end the relationship to coping with the aftermath.

Breaking up with a significant other can be a difficult and emotionally challenging decision. It is important to weigh the positive and negative aspects of the relationship before deciding to separate. Once the decision has been made, it is important to consider the potential risks of ending the relationship, both personal and general. This may include the emotional impact on both parties, the impact on shared social circles, etc.

After considering these factors, the next step is to decide on the format and location of the breakup, as well as what you will say. There are various options to consider, including breaking up in person, over the phone, or through a message. It is important to be honest and respectful when communicating your decision to end the relationship, while also considering the other person's feelings.

Before ending a relationship, it is important to take stock of the positive and negative aspects of your relationship. Consider what you want from the relationship and what you are getting from it. If you decide that it is time to break up, it is important to be aware of the potential risks, both personal and general, and to consider the best way to end the relationship.

There are many ways to break up with someone, from doing it in person to sending a text message. The best method depends on the circumstances of the relationship and the personalities of those involved. Some people prefer to do it in a public area to prevent a big scene, while others prefer to surprise their partner at home so they can leave immediately afterward. It is important to choose a method that is respectful and kind.

The aftermath of a breakup can be difficult for both the dumper and the dumpee. It is important to give yourself time and space to process your emotions and to avoid starting a new relationship until you have fully healed. Surrounding yourself with loved ones, rediscovering old routines and enjoyments, and appreciating the single life can help you cope with the aftermath of a breakup.

One important consideration when ending a relationship is the aftermath. Both parties may experience a period of depression and emotional turmoil following the breakup. It is important to have a plan in place for how to cope with these emotions, whether that includes talking to a therapist or counsellor, spending time with loved ones, or pursuing new hobbies or interests. It is also important to give oneself time and space to heal and process the breakup.

Regardless of whether you are the one initiating the breakup or the one being broken up with, breakups can be difficult for everyone involved. Developing a clear plan and understanding the breakup process can help to make the process as safe and respectful as possible. Ultimately, ending a relationship may be necessary for personal growth and happiness, but it is important to approach the process with empathy and consideration for the other person's feelings.

While breaking up with a significant other is never easy, understanding the breakup process and developing a clear plan can make it less daunting. By taking the time to assess your relationship, choosing the best method to end it, and taking care of yourself afterward, you can navigate the breakup process with grace and kindness. Remember that breakups do not equal failure and that it is natural for relationships to end. By learning from the experience, you can move forward with a newfound sense of clarity and self-awareness.

CHAPTER THREE

UNDERSTANDING HEARTBREAK AND ITS IMPACT ON US

"Heartbreak can be a catalyst for growth and change. It forces us to re-evaluate what we want, who we are, and what we are capable of." - Unknown

Heartbreak is a painful and challenging experience that most of us go through at some point in our lives. It can be caused by many things, such as the end of a romantic relationship, the loss of a loved one, or even a significant life change. No matter the cause, the aftermath of heartbreak can be devastating and can have a profound impact on our emotional and physical well-being.

In this chapter, we will explore why we suffer after heartbreak and how it affects us. Understanding the nature of heartbreak and its impact on us is essential to healing from it and moving on.

The Nature of Heartbreak

Heartbreak is a complex emotional experience that can manifest in different ways for different people. It can be a feeling of intense sadness, loneliness, anger, or betrayal. Often, heartbreak is associated with feelings of grief, as if we have lost something important to us. This can lead to a sense of emptiness or numbness that can be difficult to shake off.

What makes heartbreak particularly challenging is the fact that it can affect our physical and mental health. Studies have shown that heartbreak can lead to a range of symptoms, such as insomnia, loss of appetite, and physical pain. These symptoms are not just a coincidence - they are a reflection of the deep connection between our emotional and physical well-being.

The Impact of Heartbreak on Us

The impact of heartbreak can be long-lasting and can affect many areas of our lives. Here are some of the ways heartbreak can affect us:

1. Emotional well-being: Heartbreak can lead to intense feelings of sadness, anger, and depression. It can also make us feel insecure, anxious, and uncertain about the future.
2. Physical well-being: Heartbreak can lead to physical symptoms such as insomnia, loss of appetite, and fatigue. These symptoms can make it difficult to function in our daily lives.
3. Self-esteem: Heartbreak can damage our self-esteem and confidence. It can make us feel unworthy of love and affection and can lead to negative self-talk and self-criticism.
4. Relationships: Heartbreak can affect our ability to trust and form relationships in the future. It can also make us more guarded and less open to new experiences

Why We Suffer After Heartbreak

So why do we suffer after heartbreak? There is no single answer to this question, as the experience of heartbreak is different for everyone. However, there are some common reasons why heartbreak can be so painful:

1. Loss of attachment: When we form a close bond with someone, we become attached to them. When that bond is broken, we experience a sense of loss that can be difficult to process.
2. Fear of the unknown: Heartbreak can leave us feeling uncertain about the future. We may worry about whether we will ever find love again or whether we will be alone forever.
3. Self-blame: When a relationship ends, it is common to blame ourselves for its failure. We may feel that we were not good enough or that we did something wrong.
4. Identity crisis: When we are in a relationship, we often define ourselves in relation to our partner. When that relationship ends, we may feel lost or unsure of who we are without them.
5. Loss of routine: When we are in a relationship, we often establish a routine and become accustomed to having someone else in our lives. When the relationship ends, we may feel like we have lost that sense of stability and routine.
6. Social support: When we go through a heartbreak, we may feel like we are alone and isolated. We may not want to burden our friends and family with our problems, or we may not feel comfortable talking to them about it. This lack of social support can make it even harder to cope with the pain of heartbreak.
7. Trauma: For some people, heartbreak can be traumatic, especially if it is caused by a significant life event such as a betrayal or a sudden loss. Trauma can make it even harder to process and heal from a heartbreak and may require professional support.
8. Attachment style: Our attachment style can also impact how we experience heartbreak. People with an anxious attachment style may experience intense feelings of anxiety and fear of abandonment, while people with an avoidant attachment style may distance themselves emotionally to cope with the pain.

It is important to note that everyone's experience of heartbreak is unique, and there is no right or wrong way to feel. It is also normal to experience a range of emotions, from sadness to anger to numbness. However, if you feel like you are not able to cope with the pain of heartbreak, it may be helpful to seek professional support, such as therapy or counselling. A trained professional can help you process your emotions and develop coping strategies to help you heal and move forward.

Heartbreak is a painful and challenging experience that can have a profound impact on our emotional and physical well-being. Understanding why we suffer after heartbreak is an essential part of the healing process. By recognizing the nature of heartbreak and its impact on us, we can take the first step toward healing and move on.

CHAPTER FOUR

WE NEED BREAK: PREDICTION OF BREAKUP

"Trying to predict a breakup is like trying to solve a puzzle with missing pieces. You can make some guesses, but you'll never see the full picture until it's complete."~Mike Waltor

Heartbreak is one of the most difficult emotional experiences that one can go through. It can be a painful and overwhelming process that can take a toll on a person's mental and physical health. While heartbreak is a common occurrence, it is often unexpected and can come as a shock to those involved. In this chapter, we will discuss the signs and signals that may indicate an impending breakup, allowing you to prepare for the emotional fallout and take proactive steps to heal.

The early stages of a romantic relationship are filled with excitement and passion. However, as time goes on, some relationships may begin to show signs of strain. Predicting the end of a relationship can be a difficult task and one that is often clouded by emotions and personal biases. However, there are several factors that can provide insight into whether a relationship is likely to end. These factors can be broadly categorized into three categories: individual factors, relationship factors, and external factors.

INDIVIDUAL FACTORS

Individual factors are a critical component of predicting the end of a relationship. These factors refer to the specific characteristics and experiences of each partner in a relationship that can impact its health and longevity. Individual factors can be both personal and specific to the relationship and can include poor self-esteem, incompatible personalities, or toxic attachment styles.

Poor self-esteem is a common individual factor that can contribute to relationship problems. Individuals with low self-esteem may struggle with feelings of inadequacy, unworthiness, and self-doubt, which can negatively impact their ability to communicate effectively, establish trust, and maintain emotional intimacy in a relationship. Low self-esteem can also lead individuals to seek validation and approval from their partner, which can create an unhealthy dynamic of dependency and neediness.

Incompatible personalities are another individual factor that can contribute to relationship problems. Individuals with different personality traits may struggle to understand each other's perspectives, communicate effectively, and navigate conflicts in a healthy way. For example, if one partner is introverted and prefers alone time, while the other is extroverted and enjoys socializing, it can lead to tension and misunderstandings.

Toxic attachment styles are also individual factors that can contribute to relationship problems. Attachment styles refer to the way individuals form emotional bonds and connect with others. Individuals with a secure attachment style tend to have healthy, balanced relationships, while those with an insecure attachment style may struggle with emotional regulation, communication, and trust. Individuals with an anxious attachment style, for example, one partner may become overly dependent on their other partner, while those with an avoidant attachment style may struggle with emotional intimacy and closeness.

In addition to personal factors, individual factors can also be specific to the relationship itself. For example, if one partner has a history of infidelity, it can create a sense of distrust and insecurity that can negatively impact the health of the relationship. Similarly, if one partner has unrealistic expectations or is overly critical, it can create tension and conflict in the relationship.

Understanding individual factors is a crucial aspect of predicting the end of a relationship. By recognizing these factors and addressing them in a proactive way, individuals can potentially save their relationship or prepare for the emotional fallout of a breakup. Whether through therapy, self-reflection, or communication strategies, individuals can learn how to navigate these challenges and improve the health and longevity of their relationship

TYPE OF ATTACHMENTS

Attachment styles are a crucial component of understanding the dynamics of relationships and predicting their longevity. Attachment theory posits that early childhood experiences with caregivers shape the way individuals form emotional bonds and connect with others throughout their lives. There are four types of attachment styles based on four relationships between one's self and others: secure, fearful, preoccupied, and dismissing.

Individuals with a secure attachment style tend to have healthy, balanced relationships characterized by trust, emotional intimacy, and effective communication. Individuals with a secure attachment style have a positive model of self and others, meaning that they have a positive view of themselves and believe that others are trustworthy and reliable. They are comfortable with emotional intimacy and are able to regulate their emotions in a healthy way.

Individuals with a fearful attachment style have a negative model of both themselves and others. They struggle with emotional regulation and often feel overwhelmed by their emotions. They may avoid close relationships or feel trapped in them, as they fear abandonment and rejection. Fearful attachment styles are often a result of childhood experiences with caregivers who were inconsistent, unresponsive, or abusive.

Individuals with a preoccupied attachment style have a negative model of self and a positive model of others. They may rely heavily on others for validation and approval and struggle with self-doubt and insecurity. They tend to be overly invested in their relationships and may become clingy or demanding in an effort to maintain closeness. Preoccupied attachment styles are often a result of childhood experiences with caregivers who were inconsistent or unpredictable.

Finally, individuals with a dismissing attachment style have a positive model of self and a negative model of others. They tend to value independence and may struggle with emotional intimacy and vulnerability. They may dismiss the importance of relationships or prioritize other aspects of their lives over their romantic partners. Dismissing attachment styles are often a result of childhood experiences with caregivers who were distant or uninvolved.

Understanding attachment styles is critical for predicting the longevity of a relationship. Partners with compatible attachment styles are more likely to have healthy, balanced relationships characterized by trust, emotional intimacy, and effective communication. Conversely, partners with incompatible attachment styles may struggle to connect emotionally, communicate effectively, and establish trust.

It's important to note that attachment styles can change over time, particularly with the help of therapy and self-reflection. Individuals who have experienced trauma or difficult childhood experiences may benefit from working with a therapist to identify and address negative patterns in their relationships. Additionally, partners can work together to develop communication strategies and build trust, even if they have different attachment styles.

Understanding attachment styles is a critical aspect of predicting the longevity of a relationship. By recognizing the impact of early childhood experiences on attachment styles and working to improve communication, emotional regulation, and trust, individuals can potentially save their relationship or prepare for the emotional fallout of a breakup.

Understanding the attachment style of both partners can also be helpful in predicting how either party may react to a breakup. A partner with a secure attachment style may be able to accept the breakup and move on in a healthy way, while a partner with an insecure attachment style may struggle with feelings of rejection, abandonment, or anxiety. They may become clingy, desperate, or angry in an effort to regain the relationship or protect themselves from further emotional pain.

In some cases, understanding attachment styles can also be helpful in determining whether or not a breakup is necessary. For example, if one partner has a secure attachment style and the other has an insecure attachment style that is causing problems in the relationship, therapy or counselling may be able to help them work through these issues and potentially save the relationship.

Understanding the attachment style of both partners in a romantic relationship is an important predictor of why a relationship may not have worked out and how either party may react to the breakup. By recognizing the impact of attachment styles on relationship dynamics and emotional reactions, individuals can better prepare for the emotional fallout of a breakup and potentially work to save their relationship.

RELATIONSHIP FACTORS

Individual factors are not the only predictors of relationship stability. In addition to personal traits and tendencies, there are a variety of relationship factors that can be examined to determine the likelihood of a breakup. These factors include relational quality, interactions between partners, experiences within the relationship, cognitive representation, and structural features of relationships. In this chapter, we will explore each of these factors in detail and their impact on relationship stability.

- **Relational Quality**

One of the most important factors in predicting the end of a relationship is the overall quality of the relationship. Relational quality can be assessed by examining the degree to which partners feel connected, satisfied, and fulfilled in the relationship. Relationships that are characterized by high levels of intimacy, affection, and mutual support are more likely to be stable and long-lasting than those that are marked by conflict, mistrust, and disconnection.

- **Interactions Between Partners**

Another important factor to consider when predicting the end of a relationship is the nature of the interactions between partners. This can include the frequency and type of communication, the level of emotional expression and support, and the degree to which partners feel understood and validated by each other. Positive interactions, such as open communication and mutual validation, are associated with relationship satisfaction and longevity, while negative interactions, such as criticism and conflict, can undermine the relationship and increase the likelihood of a breakup.

- **Experiences Within the Relationship**

Experiences within the relationship can also be a predictor of relationship stability. This can include shared activities and interests, life events such as job changes or moves, and challenges such as health issues or financial problems. Relationships that are marked by positive shared experiences and the ability to weather challenges together are more likely to be stable and long-lasting.

- **Cognitive Representation**

Cognitive representation refers to the way that partners perceive and think about their relationship. This can include beliefs about the future of the relationship, perceptions of the partner's commitment and loyalty, and attitudes about the importance of the relationship. Partners who view the relationship positively and believe in its long-term potential are more likely to be satisfied and committed, while those who hold negative beliefs or doubts are more likely to experience instability and potential breakup.

- **Structural Features of Relationships**

Finally, structural features of relationships can also be a predictor of relationship stability. This can include factors such as the duration of the relationship, the level of commitment, and the presence of external stressors such as work or family demands. Relationships that are characterized by high levels of commitment, longevity, and mutual support are more likely to be stable and long-lasting.

There are a variety of relationship factors that can be examined to predict the likelihood of a breakup. By understanding the impact of these factors on relationship stability, individuals can better predict the future of their relationship and take steps to improve its longevity and quality.

RUSBULT INVESTMENT MODEL

The Rusbult Investment Model is a popular social exchange theory that provides an explanation for why some individuals choose to stay in a romantic relationship while others decide to leave. According to the model, individuals decide to stay in a relationship when they perceive that the relationship is meeting their needs for satisfaction, investment, and quality of alternatives.

Satisfaction is one of the primary factors that determine relationship stability. If a person feels happy, fulfilled, and satisfied in their relationship, they are more likely to remain committed to their partner. This satisfaction comes from the rewards of the relationship, which include love, affection, and companionship. If the rewards of the relationship outweigh the costs, then the relationship is more likely to be stable. However, if the costs of the relationship are greater than the rewards, then the individual may feel that they are putting more into the relationship than they are getting out of it.

Investment is another factor that influences relationship stability. This refers to the resources, both tangible and intangible, that individuals put into their relationships, including time, money, and emotional energy. The more resources that individuals invest in their relationships, the more committed they are likely to be to their partners. This is because investments create a sense of sunk costs, meaning that individuals are less likely to leave the relationship because they have already put so much into it.

Finally, quality of alternatives is the third factor that influences relationship stability. This refers to the availability of other potential partners who may be more attractive or suitable than one's current partner. If individuals perceive that there are high-quality alternatives available to them, then they may be more likely to leave their current relationship. On the other hand, if they perceive that there are few or no alternatives available, they may be more likely to stay in their current relationship.

the Rusbult Investment Model suggests that individuals choose to stay in a romantic relationship when they perceive that the rewards of the relationship outweigh the costs, when they have invested significant resources in the relationship, and when they perceive that there are few high-quality alternatives available to them. Conversely, individuals are more likely to leave a relationship when they perceive that the costs of the relationship outweigh the rewards, when they have made minimal investments, or when they perceive that there are many high-quality alternatives available to them.

The Rusbult Investment Model has been found to be a reliable predictor of relationship outcomes and has been used to guide interventions aimed at improving relationship satisfaction and stability. By understanding the factors that influence relationship commitment, individuals can take steps to strengthen their relationships and prevent unnecessary breakups

THE INTERDEPENDENCE THEORY

The Interdependence Theory, developed by social psychologist Harold Kelley, provides an explanation for how individuals make decisions in relationships. According to the theory, individuals make decisions based on their level of dependence on their partner and the perceived outcomes of those decisions.

The theory suggests that successful relationships require both partners to make decisions with the needs of their significant other in mind. In other words, both partners must consider the impact of their decisions on their partner and strive to meet their partner's needs, goals, and motivations. This mutual consideration creates a sense of interdependence in the relationship, which can lead to increased satisfaction and commitment.

When one or both partners do not feel that their needs have been sufficiently met, they may experience low relational satisfaction. This can occur when one partner consistently makes decisions without considering the needs of the other, leading to feelings of neglect or resentment. It can also occur when both partners make decisions that prioritize their own needs over their partner's, leading to feelings of competition or conflict.

The Interdependence Theory also suggests that the outcomes of decisions play a crucial role in relationship satisfaction. When individuals perceive that their decisions have positive outcomes for themselves and their partner, they are more likely to experience high relational satisfaction. However, when individuals perceive that their decisions have negative outcomes for themselves or their partner, they may experience low relational satisfaction or even consider ending the relationship.

Overall, the Interdependence Theory highlights the importance of mutual consideration and decision-making in relationships. When both partners prioritize meeting each other's needs and work towards shared goals, they are more likely to experience high relational satisfaction and build a strong, stable relationship. Conversely, when one or both partners consistently prioritize their own needs over their partner's or neglect their partner's needs, the relationship is more likely to experience problems and potentially end.

EXTERNAL FACTORS

External factors can have a significant impact on the stability of a romantic relationship. These factors are typically beyond the control of the partners themselves and can range from environmental stressors to the influence of others on the relationship.

One common external factor that can strain a relationship is financial struggles. Money problems can create stress, tension, and disagreements between partners, particularly if one partner is more financially responsible than the other or if they have different spending habits. Financial stress can also lead to a lack of quality time, as partners may have to work long hours to make ends meet.

Long-distance relationships can also be challenging external factors that can negatively affect a romantic relationship. The distance can make it difficult for partners to maintain a strong emotional connection, and they may struggle with feelings of loneliness or insecurity. This can be compounded if there are trust issues or other relational strains already present in the relationship.

Family attitudes can also be an external factor that can contribute to the breakup of a romantic relationship. If one partner's family does not approve of the other partner or if there are cultural or religious differences between the partners that are not accepted by their families, this can create tension and conflict. In some cases, family attitudes may even lead to the partners breaking up in order to appease their families.

Another external factor that can contribute to the breakup of a relationship is outside involvement, such as cheating or interference from friends or family. If one partner cheats on the other, it can be devastating to the relationship and can create feelings of betrayal and mistrust. Similarly, if friends or family members are actively involved in the relationship and are constantly interfering or offering unsolicited advice, this can create tension and contribute to a breakdown in communication between partners.

External factors can play a significant role in predicting the end of a romantic relationship. While individual and relationship factors are often the primary predictors of a breakup, external factors can exacerbate existing problems and create new ones. By recognizing and addressing external factors early on, partners can work together to strengthen their relationship and improve their chances of staying together.

CHAPTER FIVE

THE POWER OF ATTACHMENT THEORY AND MEMORIES IN HEALING FROM HEARTBREAK

"Our attachment to someone is often defined by the memories we create with them, the moments that leave an indelible mark on our hearts~ Harry Jamson"

One of the most critical aspects of healing from heartbreak is understanding attachment in relationships. Attachment theory is a psychological framework that explains how we form emotional bonds with others, particularly romantic partners. Understanding attachment theory can provide insight into why we experience pain and difficulty in letting go after a breakup.

Attachment theory posits that our early childhood experiences with our primary caregivers shape our attachment styles. These attachment styles are then carried into our adult romantic relationships. There are three primary attachment styles: secure, anxious-ambivalent, and avoidant.

Individuals with a secure attachment style tend to have positive views of themselves and others. They are comfortable with intimacy and are able to communicate their needs and emotions effectively. These individuals tend to have stable, fulfilling relationships.

In contrast, individuals with an anxious-ambivalent attachment style tend to have negative views of themselves and positive views of others. They may cling to their partners and have a strong fear of abandonment. These individuals tend to experience intense emotional highs and lows in their relationships.

Finally, individuals with an avoidant attachment style tend to have negative views of both themselves and others. They may avoid intimacy and have difficulty expressing their emotions. These individuals tend to prioritize independence and self-sufficiency over the emotional connection.

Understanding your own attachment style can help you better comprehend why you may be struggling to move on after a breakup. For example, if you have an anxious-ambivalent attachment style, you may find yourself obsessing over your ex-partner and struggling to let go. Recognizing this attachment style and working on developing a more secure attachment style can help you build healthier, more fulfilling relationships in the future.

In addition to understanding your own attachment style, it's essential to recognize the attachment style of your ex-partner. If your ex had an avoidant attachment style, they may have difficulty expressing their emotions and may have been emotionally distant throughout the relationship. On the other hand, if your ex had an anxious-ambivalent attachment style, they may have been overly clingy and dependent on you.

Understanding your ex-partner's attachment style can help you gain insight into their behaviour during the relationship and after the breakup. It can also provide a framework for understanding why the relationship may have ended and how to avoid similar issues in future relationships.

Attachment theory provides a valuable framework for understanding our emotional bonds with others, particularly in romantic relationships. Understanding your own attachment style and that of your ex-partner can provide insight into the dynamics of the relationship and aid in the healing process after a heartbreak.

Memories are an inevitable part of any relationship, and after a breakup, they can be a source of pain, comfort, or both. Memories can take many forms, from shared experiences and inside jokes to photographs and mementos. While it can be difficult to let go of the memories of a past relationship, they can also provide an opportunity for healing and growth.

- **The Good Memories:**

One of the reasons it can be so hard to move on after a breakup is the loss of the good memories. The moments of joy, love, and happiness that were shared can feel like they have been erased, leaving only the pain and heartbreak. However, it is important to remember that those memories are still there and can be cherished, even if the relationship has ended. Rather than trying to forget those moments, it can be helpful to acknowledge and honour them as a part of your personal history. This can include looking through old photos, revisiting places that hold special meaning, or simply taking time to reflect on the positive experiences shared.

- **The Bad Memories:**

Along with the good memories, there are often bad memories that come up after a breakup. These can include arguments, hurtful words, and moments of betrayal or disappointment. These memories can be particularly painful, and it can be tempting to dwell on them, replaying the hurtful moments over and over in your mind. However, holding onto these memories can prevent healing and growth. Instead, it can be helpful to acknowledge these memories, process the emotions associated with them, and then work to let them go. This can include talking to a therapist, journaling, or finding healthy ways to express your emotions, such as through exercise or creative outlets.

The Healing Power of Memories:

While memories can be a source of pain, they can also be a powerful tool for healing. By reflecting on the good memories, it is possible to find gratitude for the positive experiences that were shared, even if the relationship ended. By acknowledging the bad memories, it is possible to learn from the mistakes made and to grow as a person. Memories can also serve as a reminder of the personal strengths and qualities that were present in the relationship, and can be used as a foundation for future relationships.

Memories are an integral part of any relationship, and after a breakup, they can be both a source of pain and a source of healing. By acknowledging and honouring the good memories, processing the bad memories, and finding gratitude for the lessons learned, it is possible to move forward after a heartbreak with a greater sense of peace and personal growth.

CHAPTER SIX

THIS IS TOXIC

"Being in a toxic relationship is like standing in a room full of poison; the longer you stay, the more it damages your health and wellbeing.~Niomi Jack"

How do you know whether you are satisfied with your romantic relationship? Assessing relational satisfaction is an important aspect of predicting the longevity of a romantic relationship. However, it can be challenging to measure as relationships are highly personal and subjective experiences that can differ greatly from one individual to another. Despite these challenges, there are several methods for measuring relational satisfaction that can be used to predict the future status of a relationship.

One approach is to measure satisfaction at a single point in time through surveys or ask questions. These surveys typically ask questions that are designed to gauge how satisfied individuals are with their romantic relationships. The answers to these questions can then be scored and used to calculate an overall satisfaction rating. While this approach is relatively easy to administer, it is important to note that satisfaction levels can fluctuate over time and that a single point-in-time measure may not be a reliable predictor of future outcomes.

Another approach is to measure satisfaction between two time periods. This method involves administering surveys or interviews at two different points in time, such as at the beginning and end of a relationship. By comparing the satisfaction levels between these two time periods, we can gain insight into how the relationship has changed over time and predict future outcomes based on these changes.

It is also important to consider who is being assessed for satisfaction. In some cases, both partners in a relationship may be assessed individually. By comparing the satisfaction levels of each partner, we can gain insight into how the relationship is perceived by each individual and predict how these perceptions may impact future outcomes.

Furthermore, it is important to understand that satisfaction is not a one-dimensional concept. There are often look at multiple dimensions of satisfaction, including emotional, physical, and sexual satisfaction. By examining satisfaction across these different dimensions, we can gain a more comprehensive understanding of how satisfied individuals are with their romantic relationship.

Ultimately, measuring relational satisfaction is an important tool for predicting the future status of a romantic relationship. While there are several methods for measuring satisfaction, it is important to use a comprehensive approach that considers multiple dimensions of satisfaction and assesses both partners in the relationship. By gaining a deeper understanding of satisfaction levels, individuals can make more informed decisions about the future of their relationship and take steps to improve relational satisfaction if necessary.

RELATIONAL DISSATISFACTION

When a relationship is not meeting one's needs and expectations, relational dissatisfaction is likely to occur. This can manifest in a variety of ways, such as feelings of unhappiness, disappointment, and frustration. Ignoring these signs can lead to further relationship problems and ultimately, a breakup.

While the decision to end a relationship may be necessary for one's emotional well-being, it also comes with its own set of risks and challenges. The period following a breakup can be filled with uncertainty, fear, and emotional turmoil. It's important to be aware of these risks and take steps to prepare for them.

One of the most common risks following a breakup is conflict. Feelings of anger, resentment, and hurt can lead to disagreements and arguments between both parties. This can result in a toxic and hostile environment that can be detrimental to both individuals' emotional health. It's important to approach post-breakup communication and interactions with care, respect, and empathy.

Another risk is emotional pain. The end of a relationship can be a traumatic experience that can cause deep emotional pain and distress. It's normal to experience a range of emotions, such as sadness, loneliness, and grief. It's important to seek support from friends, family, or a therapist to help manage these emotions and navigate through the healing process.

In addition, there is a risk of losing mutual friends or support systems. Many couples share a social circle or support network, and ending a relationship can result in losing these connections. It's important to maintain healthy relationships with these individuals and avoid putting them in a position where they feel like they have to choose sides.

Finally, there is the risk of falling into old patterns or making impulsive decisions. After a breakup, it's common to feel vulnerable and seek comfort in familiar or unhealthy behaviours. It's important to recognize these patterns and make conscious decisions to break free from them.

relational dissatisfaction is a clear indication that a relationship is heading toward its end. However, it's important to be aware of the risks that come with a breakup and take steps to prepare for them. This includes managing conflict, seeking support, maintaining healthy relationships, and avoiding old patterns. With time and effort, it is possible to heal from the pain of a breakup and move forward towards a healthier and happier future.

PREDICTING AND COPING WITH POST-BREAKUP RISKS AND REACTIONS

Breakups are difficult for everyone involved, regardless of whether you are the one initiating the split or the one being dumped. The aftermath of a breakup can be particularly challenging, and studies have shown that certain factors can predict how individuals will react to a breakup. Demographic variables such as age and gender, as well as characteristics of the relationship such as duration and personal history, and personality factors such as attachment style or habits, can all play a role in determining how someone will respond to a breakup.

While nobody expects to experience a breakup when entering into a romantic partnership, it is important to be prepared for the aftermath of a split. The grieving process typically involves feelings of depression, anger, sadness, and despair, and it is important to acknowledge and address these emotions. According to research conducted by Dr. Tiffany Field in 2011, common symptoms of a breakup include sleep disturbances and intrusive thoughts, as well as attempts to control these thoughts.

While these symptoms can vary across cultures and individuals, it is important to be aware of the potential challenges that can arise after a breakup. In some cases, more serious post-breakup symptoms can occur, including "Broken Heart" syndrome and endocrine/immunity dysfunction. It is important to seek support from friends, family, or a therapist during this difficult time, and to take steps to prioritize self-care and emotional well-being. By recognizing the potential risks and challenges of a breakup and taking proactive steps to address them, individuals can begin to heal and move forward after the end of a relationship.

Sleepless Nights and Broken Hearts: The Impact of Breakups on Sleep Patterns and Heart Health

Breakups can have a significant impact on an individual's sleep patterns. Research conducted by Dr. Tiffany Field shows that as many as 43% of test subjects experience onset insomnia, which is connected to night-time ruminations about the loss of the relationship. Intrusive thoughts are also commonly reported, causing high levels of anxiety and making it difficult for many to fall asleep.

Moreover, initiating a breakup can have potential morbidity factors, which include broken heart syndrome or Takotsubo cardiomyopathy. Broken heart syndrome causes overwhelming heart attack-like symptoms, which can lead to heart failure. Although it is very rare and mostly seen in elderly individuals, it can also occur due to the stress of an emotional breakup. Women are more likely to suffer from broken heart syndrome than men, and it is a condition that is most prominent in older generations with pre-existing conditions.

Takotsubo cardiomyopathy, also known as broken heart syndrome, is a rare but serious condition that can occur following a highly stressful event, such as an emotional breakup or the loss of a loved one. The condition is characterized by sudden and severe chest pain, shortness of breath, and other symptoms that are similar to those of a heart attack.

Broken heart syndrome is caused by a surge of stress hormones, such as adrenaline and cortisol, which can temporarily disrupt the normal functioning of the heart muscle. Unlike a typical heart attack, broken heart syndrome does not involve a blockage in the coronary arteries. Instead, the heart muscle becomes weakened and unable to pump blood effectively, leading to symptoms that are similar to those of a heart attack.

The condition is named after the Japanese word "takotsubo," which means "octopus pot." This is because the shape of the heart during a broken heart syndrome episode resembles a pot used to trap octopuses.

While broken heart syndrome is a serious condition, it is usually reversible with treatment. Most people recover within a few weeks or months with rest and medications to help manage symptoms. However, it is important to seek medical attention immediately if you experience symptoms of broken heart syndrome, as the condition can be life-threatening in some cases.

THE DETERRENT EFFECT IN ROMANTIC RELATIONSHIPS

The decision to end a romantic relationship is not always an easy one, and individuals may experience various emotions and thought processes before reaching that conclusion. Once an individual decides to end a relationship, they may experience a phenomenon known as "looking through rose-coloured glasses". This can lead to the individual overlooking the negative aspects of the relationship and focusing only on the positive memories and qualities of their partner. This can cause some individuals to change their minds about ending the relationship, and they may choose to continue in the relationship.

This phenomenon is related to the concept of deterrence, where obstacles to intense emotions can produce paradoxical effects on one's emotions. This means that the obstacles to ending a relationship can outweigh the individual's desire to end the relationship, causing the emotion to drop to a minimum level of intensity. In this case, individuals may be willing to overlook their desire to end the relationship because they fear loneliness or abandonment. They may believe that a broken relationship is better than being alone and hope that the relationship can be fixed.

However, this can lead to negative addictive behaviours used as a distraction, such as binge eating or retail therapy. The individual may also view the dumped as their support system and not want to lose that support. The fear of losing this support may cause the dumper to hold onto the relationship, even if it is no longer healthy or fulfilling.

The decision to end a romantic relationship can be a difficult one, and individuals may experience various emotions and thought processes before reaching that conclusion. Once the decision has been made, the individual may experience a phenomenon known as "looking through rose-coloured glasses", where they focus only on the positive aspects of the relationship and overlook the negative aspects. This can lead to individuals changing their minds about ending the relationship and choosing to continue in the relationship. The fear of loneliness or abandonment can be a strong deterrent for ending a relationship, and may cause individuals to hold onto the relationship even if it is no longer healthy or fulfilling.

CHAPTER SEVEN

NAVIGATING RELATIONSHIPS: RECOGNIZING RED AND GREEN FLAGS

When we enter into a new relationship, it's common to feel a sense of excitement and hope for the future. However, it's important to be aware of potential red flags that could signal an unhealthy relationship. At the same time, we should also keep an eye out for green flags that indicate a positive and healthy partnership.

Entering into a new relationship can be an exciting time filled with hope for a happy future. However, it's important to be aware of potential red flags that could signal an unhealthy relationship. It's equally important to keep an eye out for green flags that indicate a positive and healthy partnership. This book aims to provide readers with a comprehensive guide to recognizing red and green flags in relationships, and how to navigate them for a fulfilling and healthy partnership.

Red Flags

Red flags are warning signs that suggest a relationship may not be healthy or sustainable. While every relationship is different, there are a few common red flags to watch out for:

1. Lack of Communication: Communication is key to any healthy relationship. If your partner consistently avoids communication or refuses to engage in difficult conversations, it may be a sign of underlying issues.
2. Control Issues: If your partner tries to control your behaviour, such as telling you what to wear, where to go, or who to spend time with, it's a major red flag.
3. Disrespect: If your partner disrespects your opinions, feelings, or boundaries, it's a clear sign that they don't value you as a person.
4. Dishonesty: Trust is essential to any relationship, and dishonesty can quickly erode that trust. If your partner lies to you or withholds important information, it's a major red flag.
5. Manipulation: If your partner uses guilt, fear, or other tactics to get their way, it's a sign of manipulation and a potential red flag.

Green Flags

Green flags are positive signs that suggest a relationship is healthy and supportive. Here are a few common green flags to look out for:

1. Respect: A healthy relationship is built on mutual respect. If your partner consistently shows you respect, listens to your opinions, and values your boundaries, it's a good sign.
2. Support: In a healthy relationship, partners support each other's goals and dreams. If your partner encourages you to pursue your passions and provides emotional support when you need it, it's a positive green flag.
3. Open Communication: Healthy communication is key to any relationship, and a partner who is willing to engage in difficult conversations and listen to your perspective is a good sign.
4. Honesty: Honesty and trust go hand in hand. A partner who is honest with you, even when it's difficult, is a green flag.
5. Compromise: A healthy relationship requires compromise and a willingness to work together. If your partner is willing to find

solutions that work for both of you, it's a positive sign.

Disrespectful Behaviours: Recognizing and Addressing Them

we dive into the topic of disrespectful behaviours in relationships. Disrespectful behaviours can include name-calling, belittling, invalidating someone's feelings, and other forms of verbal abuse. We also explore non-verbal disrespectful behaviours such as ignoring someone, rolling your eyes, or giving the silent treatment.

It's important to recognize these behaviours in our own relationships and to understand how they can affect us emotionally and psychologically. We provide tips on how to address disrespectful behaviours in a constructive way, such as setting boundaries, using "I" statements, and seeking support from a therapist or trusted friend.

Building Healthy Communication Habits

we focus on the importance of healthy communication habits in relationships. We discuss the role of active listening, the power of empathy, and the importance of expressing ourselves clearly and respectfully.

We provide practical tips for building healthy communication habits, such as setting aside dedicated time for communication, avoiding distractions, and practicing "active listening" by repeating what your partner has said to ensure understanding.

We also discuss how to navigate difficult conversations, such as disagreements or conflicts, in a healthy and productive way. This includes avoiding blame and criticism, using "I" statements, and seeking common ground to find solutions that work for both partners.

Being aware of both red flags and green flags can help us navigate our relationships more effectively. By paying attention to warning signs and seeking out positive signs, we can build healthy and fulfilling partnerships. Remember that every relationship is unique, and it's up to you to decide what's best for your own wellbeing.

Navigating relationships can be challenging, but by recognizing red and green flags, communicating effectively, and working together as a team, readers can build healthy and fulfilling partnerships. This book aims to provide readers with the tools and knowledge they need to navigate relationships with confidence and build strong and lasting connections with their partners.

CHAPTER EIGHT

WHY THIS HURT SO MUCH

"The reason it hurts so much to seperate is beacuse are souls are conected`~Niclolas Sparks"

Breakups can be one of the most painful experiences a person can go through. The emotional pain can be so intense that it can feel like physical pain, and it can be difficult to understand why it hurts so much. The reality is that there are a variety of reasons why a breakup can be so painful.

Heartbreak is a painful experience that many of us have gone through at some point in our lives. It can leave us feeling lost, sad, and overwhelmed with emotions that seem impossible to deal with. So, why does heartbreak hurt so much?

It's important to remember that it's normal to feel a range of emotions after a breakup. It's okay to feel sad, angry, or confused. It's also okay to take time to grieve the loss of the relationship. Healing from a breakup takes time, and it's important to be patient with yourself and take care of your emotional needs.

One reason is that we become emotionally attached to our partners. Over time, we develop deep emotional bonds with them, and those bonds can be difficult to break. When a relationship ends, it can feel like we are losing a part of ourselves. This loss can trigger feelings of grief, sadness, and loneliness.

Another reason why breakups hurt so much is that they often represent a significant change in our lives. Our partner may have been a constant in our lives for years, and the breakup can disrupt our sense of stability and security. We may also have to face the prospect of being alone, which can be scary and overwhelming.

In addition, breakups can bring up a lot of unresolved emotions and issues. We may find ourselves questioning our self-worth, feeling angry or resentful towards our partner, or grappling with feelings of guilt or regret. These emotions can be intense and overwhelming, and it can take time to process them.

Another reason is that we have formed a deep emotional attachment to our partner. This attachment is formed through shared experiences, emotional intimacy, and a sense of security and comfort that comes with being in a relationship. When the relationship ends, this attachment is suddenly severed, leaving us feeling like we have lost a part of ourselves. We may also experience a sense of betrayal, particularly if the breakup was unexpected or unwanted.

Another reason why heartbreak hurts so much is that it can activate our fear of abandonment. This fear is often rooted in our childhood experiences and can be triggered by the end of a relationship. We may feel like we are not good enough or that we are unlovable, which can further exacerbate our pain and make it difficult to move on.

Furthermore, heartbreak can also activate our stress response system, leading to physical and emotional symptoms such as anxiety, depression, and insomnia. This is because the loss of a relationship can be perceived as a threat to our survival, triggering our fight-or-flight response.

It is important to acknowledge and process these feelings of pain and loss rather than trying to suppress or ignore them. This can be done through self-care practices such as exercise, meditation, and therapy. It is also important to surround ourselves with supportive friends and family who can provide a listening ear and a shoulder to lean on.

While heartbreak may feel unbearable in the moment, it is important to remember that time heals all wounds. With time, self-care, and support, we can move through the pain of heartbreak and emerge stronger and more resilient on the other side.

Breakups hurt so much because they represent a loss of emotional attachment, a significant change in our lives, and a range of unresolved emotions and issues. It's important to acknowledge and validate these feelings in order to begin the healing process. With time, patience, and self-care, it is possible to move on from a breakup and find happiness and fulfilment in the future.

CHAPTER NINE

CAN WE STILL BE FRIENDS?

One of the most common questions people ask themselves after a breakup is, "Can we still be friends?" It's natural to want to maintain some level of connection with someone you were once close to, but it's not always the best idea. Whether or not you can be friends with your ex depends on a number of factors, including the nature of your relationship, how the breakup occurred, and your own personal feelings.

First and foremost, it's important to consider why you want to be friends with your ex. Are you genuinely interested in maintaining a platonic relationship, or are you hoping to keep the possibility of getting back together open? If it's the latter, then it's probably best to take some time apart and work on healing yourself before trying to reconnect.

Assuming you genuinely want to be friends, the next step is to assess the state of your relationship. Were you and your ex able to communicate effectively and resolve conflicts in a healthy way? Or did your relationship have a lot of drama and turmoil? If it was the latter, then it may be best to cut ties entirely in order to protect your own mental health.

Another important factor to consider is how the breakup occurred. If one person ended the relationship while the other still had strong feelings, then it may be difficult to transition to a platonic friendship right away. It's important to be respectful of each other's feelings and give each other space to process the breakup.

On the other hand, if the breakup was mutual or if you both agree that a romantic relationship is no longer on the table, then it may be possible to transition to a friendship. However, it's important to set boundaries and establish clear expectations for the nature of your relationship. Will you still hang out one-on-one, or only in group settings? Will you continue to talk about personal matters, or keep the conversation light and casual?

Ultimately, whether or not you can be friends with your ex depends on the specific circumstances of your relationship and breakup. It's important to be honest with yourself about your own feelings and motivations, and to prioritize your own mental health and well-being above all else. If you do decide to try and maintain a friendship, approach it with open communication and clear boundaries, and be prepared to give each other space if needed.

When it comes to post-breakup friendships, it's important to consider whether or not it's truly possible to remain friends with an ex-partner. While it may seem like a good idea in theory, it's not always the best choice for everyone involved.

For some, maintaining a friendship with an ex can be a source of comfort and support during the healing process. However, for others, it can be a constant reminder of the pain and hurt from the relationship. It's important to be honest with yourself about whether or not you can handle being friends with your ex, and to communicate openly with them about your feelings.

If both parties are open to remaining friends, it's important to establish boundaries and expectations. It's essential to ensure that both people are on the same page and that the friendship doesn't cross any boundaries that could cause further emotional distress.

It's also important to acknowledge that a post-breakup friendship may not be possible or healthy in all situations. If the relationship ended due to betrayal or abuse, attempting to maintain a friendship could be dangerous and hinder the healing process. It's important to prioritize your own well-being and safety above any desire to maintain a friendship.

Ultimately, the decision to remain friends with an ex-partner is a personal one, and there is no right answer. It's important to take time to reflect on your own feelings and needs, and to communicate openly and honestly with your ex about your intentions. Remember, healing from a breakup takes time, and it's important to prioritize self-care and self-love throughout the process.

CHAPTER TEN

THE ROLE OF TECHNOLOGY IN BREAKUPS

In today's modern world, technology plays a significant role in every aspect of our lives, including romantic relationships. With the advent of social media, texting, and email, breaking up with someone has become easier and more convenient than ever before. However, this method of ending a relationship is not always the preferred method, especially for the person being broken up with.

Dr. Ilana Gershon's research in 2008 found that younger generations (18-22) tend to find phone calls or online messages more appropriate for breaking up than older generations, especially if it is a long-distance relationship. However, more recent data suggests that abrupt or decreased communication can lead to confusion about the relationship status for one or both partners.

While mediated communication may be appealing to young people for flirting and other purposes, Meenagh suggests that there are no set rules for breaking up with someone. It is ultimately up to the individual terminating the relationship to decide the when, where, and why.

Although technology can be useful in initiating, intensifying, and communicating in a romantic relationship, it is best to avoid using it to break up with someone. Face-to-face communication is still the most appropriate way to terminate a relationship, as it allows for non-verbal cues and a more nuanced understanding of the situation.

There may not be a set of rules for breaking up with someone, there are certainly ways to do it that are more considerate and respectful to the other person's feelings. The Cornell University study mentioned above found that people feel the most hurt when being rejected in favour of another person, which highlights the importance of being honest and transparent with your partner during a breakup.

In terms of mediated breakups, while younger generations may find it more acceptable to use technology to end a relationship, it is still important to consider the potential for confusion and misunderstandings that can arise from mediated communication. When communication ends abruptly or decreases, there is a risk of confusion about the relationship status for one or both partners. This is why, as the author of a book on healing from heartbreak, I would caution against using technology as a means of ending a romantic relationship unless absolutely necessary.

Ultimately, the best way to end a romantic relationship is through open and honest communication, even if that means having an uncomfortable conversation in person. While it may be tempting to avoid confrontation by using technology, doing so can ultimately cause more harm than good. In the end, the most important thing is to treat your partner with kindness and respect, even when ending the relationship.

Technology has changed the way we communicate and interact with each other, including in romantic relationships. While mediated communication may be acceptable to some, it is still best to end a relationship in person to avoid confusion and hurt feelings. It is also important to refrain from post-relationship contact and tracking behaviours to allow both individuals to move on and heal from the breakup.

CHAPTER ELEVEN

UNDERSTANDING THE DIFFERENCE BETWEEN NEEDS AND NEEDINESS: BUILDING HEALTHY RELATIONSHIPS AND HEALING FROM HEARTBREAK

I believe that understanding the difference between needs and neediness is crucial for healing from heartbreak and for building healthy relationships in the future. When we confuse our needs with the need for a specific person or action, we put ourselves in a vulnerable position where our happiness and wellbeing are dependent on external factors. This can lead to feelings of desperation and neediness, which can ultimately sabotage our relationships.

Instead, it's important to recognize that we all have valid needs that must be met in order for us to thrive as individuals. Whether it's the need for love, affection, or community, these needs are an essential part of our human experience. However, it's up to us to take responsibility for getting these needs met, rather than relying on others to fulfil them.

This is not to say that we should never rely on others for support or comfort. Seeking help and support from loved ones is an important part of the healing process. However, when we expect others to fulfil all of our needs, we give away our power and put ourselves in a position of neediness.

By taking responsibility for our own needs, we empower ourselves to build strong and healthy relationships based on mutual respect and support. It allows us to avoid the trap of neediness and to approach

I believe that the concept of needs versus neediness is an important one to explore when it comes to healing from heartbreak. It's natural to feel hurt and vulnerable after a relationship ends, but it's important to remember that we are all responsible for our own happiness and wellbeing.

One way to do this is to create a support system of friends, family, and professionals who can help us meet our needs. Whether it's seeking out a therapist to work through our emotions or joining a social group to meet new people, there are many ways to build a fulfilling life outside of a romantic relationship.

As humans, we all have needs, and it's essential to recognize them and take responsibility for fulfilling them. However, there is a big difference between having needs and being needy in a relationship. Being needy often stems from insecurity, fear of abandonment, and a deep desire to be loved and reassured constantly.

When we are needy, we tend to rely heavily on our partner to manage our emotions, regulate our self-worth, and fulfil our needs. We may project our insecurities onto our partner, seeking constant validation and attention, or try to control or smother them, ultimately pushing them away instead of creating a healthy connection.

In contrast, having needs means recognizing what we need to feel fulfilled and happy in a relationship while taking personal responsibility for meeting those needs. It involves self-reflection, examining our triggers, and building independence, hobbies, and goals outside of the relationship to support ourselves and our partner.

When we are true to ourselves and feel comfortable discussing our concerns and insecurities with our partner, we can create a healthy, secure, and fulfilling relationship. We can encourage each other to pursue our passions and support each other's growth and independence while respecting each other's boundaries and needs.

the key difference between neediness and having needs is personal responsibility. By taking responsibility for meeting our needs while respecting our partner's needs, we can build a healthy and fulfilling relationship that supports our growth and happiness.

Having need

Having needs is an important part of being human. It means acknowledging that we have emotional, physical, and psychological requirements that need to be met for us to feel fulfilled and content in life. This includes basic needs such as safety, security, love, and affection, as well as more complex needs such as intellectual stimulation, creative expression, and a sense of purpose.

Having needs is not the same as being needy. Unlike neediness, having needs is about taking ownership of our own emotional well-being and recognizing that it's our responsibility to communicate our needs to our partner in a healthy and mature way.

For instance, if we need more quality time with our partner, we can express this need without making them feel guilty or responsible for our happiness. We can have an open and honest conversation about our feelings, and work together to find a solution that works for both of us.

Having needs also means recognizing that our partner has needs of their own, and being willing to support and nurture them in their quest for happiness and fulfilment. It's a two-way street that requires mutual respect, empathy, and a commitment to emotional growth and well-being.

Having needs is a natural and healthy part of being human. It allows us to build strong, fulfilling relationships based on mutual respect, trust, and emotional intimacy. By owning our needs and communicating them in a healthy and mature way, we can build deeper connections with our partner and create a more fulfilling and satisfying life together.

How we overcorrect

Overcorrecting can result in a number of negative consequences. For one, we may end up feeling unfulfilled or resentful in relationships because our needs are not being met. We may also struggle with feelings of inadequacy or unworthiness, believing that we don't deserve to have our needs met or that we are not good enough to ask for what we want.

Overcorrecting can also lead to a lack of self-awareness and self-care. When we neglect our needs, we may not even be aware of what we want or need in a relationship, making it difficult to communicate those needs to our partner. This can lead to misunderstandings, frustration, and conflict.

Additionally, when we overcorrect, we may attract partners who are not a good match for us. People who are drawn to those who overcompensate or suppress their needs are often attracted to the idea of having control or power in the relationship. This can lead to unhealthy dynamics where one person is constantly giving while the other takes, leading to resentment and burnout.

Ultimately, it's important to strike a balance between being true to our needs and respecting the needs of our partner. By doing so, we can create healthier, more fulfilling relationships that allow us to grow and thrive as individuals.

Your responsibility in a relationship

As an individual in a relationship, it is important to take responsibility for your own needs and emotions. You cannot expect your partner to fulfil all of your needs, as they are their own person with their own needs and desires.

It is important to communicate your needs to your partner in a clear and respectful way. This means being vulnerable and honest about what you need to feel fulfilled and happy in the relationship.

It is also important to actively work on your own personal growth and development outside of the relationship. This means pursuing your own interests and hobbies, taking care of your physical and mental health, and cultivating relationships with friends and family.

In addition, taking responsibility in a relationship means being willing to work through conflicts and challenges together. It means being willing to listen to your partner's perspective, acknowledging your own mistakes, and working towards a resolution that benefits both of you.

Ultimately, your responsibility in a relationship is to contribute to the growth and happiness of both yourself and your partner. By communicating your needs, taking care of your own well-being, and working together through challenges, you can build a strong and fulfilling relationship.

How to get your needs met?

In any relationship, whether it be romantic, familial, or platonic, it is important to have your needs met. However, many people struggle to communicate their needs effectively and end up feeling unfulfilled or resentful. In this context, this topic discusses how to get your needs met in a relationship. It covers the importance of developing a fulfilling life outside of a relationship, identifying your needs, communicating them unapologetically, choosing a partner who can meet your needs, and walking away if necessary. By following these guidelines, individuals can build healthy, fulfilling relationships with partners who respect and support their needs

There is no point in being in a relationship where you can't be honest and open about what you need.

1. Develop a fulfilling life: It is important to have a fulfilling life outside of a relationship. No matter how hard you try, if you don't have a life that fills you outside of a relationship, the relationship will be doomed. Having interests, hobbies, and goals that bring you joy and purpose can help you maintain a healthy balance and avoid putting too much pressure on the relationship to fulfil all your needs.

2. Figure out what brings you joy outside of relationships: Identifying what brings you joy and fulfilment outside of relationships can help you narrow down the list of what's truly important to you in a partner. No one person can meet all of your needs, and putting that kind of pressure on them is unfair. Prioritizing what's most important to you can help you choose a partner who aligns with those values and interests.

3. Identify your needs: Understanding what you need in a relationship is crucial to getting those needs met. This involves considering how you like to give and receive love, what makes you feel safe and comfortable, your non-negotiables and deal breakers, and the top three things you can't live without in a relationship. Once you have identified your needs, you can communicate them to your partner and work together to ensure they are met.

4. Practice owning your needs unapologetically and communicating them directly: It's important to communicate your needs directly and unapologetically. This involves being honest with yourself and your partner about what you need in the relationship. If you're not sure what your needs are, it's okay to let your partner know you're sorting through it and

committed to communicating when you have a better understanding.

5. Choose a partner who can meet your needs: Choosing a partner who can meet your needs involves finding someone whose actions match their words and demonstrates consistency and commitment. Trusting someone when they show you they are low-effort, emotionally unavailable, or inconsistent can lead to disappointment and hurt. When choosing a partner, it's important to prioritize someone who can meet your needs and aligns with your values.

6. Walk away if someone shows you they can't or won't meet you: If your partner consistently fails to meet your needs, it's important to recognize that they may not be the right person for you. Wasting time hoping someone will eventually change can lead to disappointment and resentment. Walking away from a relationship where your needs are not being met can be difficult but necessary for your well-being. Knowing your worth and taking care of yourself is crucial in finding a fulfilling and healthy relationship.

ITS NOT YOU ITS ME: THE BREAKUP

Breaking up can be one of the most difficult experiences in life, and it's not uncommon to feel lost, confused, and hurt after a relationship ends. In the aftermath of a breakup, it's easy to blame oneself and wonder what went wrong. But the truth is, it's not always about us.

One of the most common phrases uttered during a breakup is "It's not you, it's me." While it may seem like a cliché, there's often a lot of truth behind those words. Sometimes, relationships simply run their course, and it's nobody's fault. Other times, there may be issues within the other person that have nothing to do with us.

It's important to remember that a breakup doesn't define who we are as individuals. We're all flawed and imperfect, and relationships are complex. Even if the breakup was a result of our actions, it's essential to recognize that we're not defined by our mistakes.

When we hear the phrase "It's not you, it's me," it can be challenging to accept. We may feel like we've been rejected, or we may feel like we've done something wrong. But in reality, it's an opportunity for growth and self-reflection.

In some cases, the "It's not you, it's me" explanation can be frustratingly vague and unsatisfying. It's natural to want to understand what went wrong and to look for ways to improve yourself or the relationship. However, it's important to recognize that sometimes, a breakup simply means that two people are no longer compatible, and it's not necessarily anyone's fault.

Instead of dwelling on what you could have done differently or how you could have been a better partner, try to focus on accepting the reality of the situation. Recognize that sometimes, relationships simply don't work out, and that's okay. It's also important to resist the temptation to blame yourself or your ex for the breakup. This kind of thinking can be counterproductive and can prevent you from moving on.

Instead, try to see the breakup as an opportunity for growth and self-reflection. Take some time to think about what you want and need in a relationship, and what you can offer to a partner. Use this time to work on yourself, to pursue your own interests, and to connect with friends and family.

Remember, healing from a breakup takes time. It's okay to feel sad, angry, or confused in the aftermath of a breakup. Allow yourself to feel these emotions and to grieve the end of the relationship. But also try to stay focused on the future, and on the possibility of new relationships and new beginnings. With time and effort, you will heal from this breakup and move forward with renewed strength and resilience.

Instead of dwelling on the breakup, it's crucial to take the time to reflect on the relationship as a whole. What did we learn? What can we do differently in future relationships? Taking the time to process the breakup and learn from it can help us move forward and avoid making the same mistakes in the future.

A breakup is never easy, but it's important to remember that it's not always about us. Sometimes, relationships simply don't work out, and that's okay. It's an opportunity for growth and self-reflection, and it's a chance to learn from our mistakes and become better versions of ourselves. Remember, it's not you, it's not me - it's just life.

Navigating Face Threats During Heartbreak: Understanding the Impact of Breakups on Identity.

The aftermath of a breakup can be particularly challenging for individuals as they navigate through the emotional turmoil that arises from ending a romantic relationship. Not only does the pain of the breakup linger for some time, but individuals also struggle with the changes that occur to their identity in the aftermath. This is because romantic relationships can significantly shape an individual's sense of self and the role they play in a partnership.

According to Kunkel et al. (2003), there are two distinct faces that individuals have: a positive face, which desires approval from others, and a negative face, which seeks autonomy from constraint. The study conducted by Kunkel et al. highlights how breakups challenge these faces and can lead to face threats. The study identified eight face threats that were determined to strongly correlate with the three goals of initiating, intensifying, and terminating romantic relationships.

1. The first face threat, "pressuring other," is particularly relevant when it comes to ending a relationship. This is because individuals who are initiating the breakup may feel pressure to end things in a way that doesn't hurt their partner or cause them to feel attacked.
2. The second face threat, "preclude future relationships," can arise when individuals fear that ending the current relationship may limit their chances of finding love in the future.
3. The third face threat, "lose desirable current relationship," can be particularly challenging for individuals who are on the receiving end of the breakup. This is because the end of the relationship may threaten their positive face and cause them to question their self-worth.
4. The fourth face threat, "make other appear inadequate," can arise when individuals feel the need to justify the breakup by pointing out their partner's flaws.

5. The fifth face threat, "appear attractive," highlights how individuals may feel pressure to maintain their appearance and present themselves in a positive light during and after the breakup.
6. The sixth face threat, "not appear too forward," may arise when individuals fear that they are being too pushy or aggressive in their attempts to initiate or end a relationship.
7. The seventh face threat, "not look overly dependent," highlights how individuals may fear being viewed as too reliant on their partner or too needy.
8. The eighth face threat, "not look insensitive," highlights how individuals may fear being viewed as callous or insensitive during and after the breakup.

Overall, understanding the different face threats that can arise during a breakup can help individuals navigate the emotional challenges that come with ending a romantic relationship. By being aware of these potential face threats, individuals can take steps to address them and ensure that the breakup is handled in a way that is respectful, compassionate, and mindful of the other person's feelings.

It's important to note that the face threats identified in the study by Kunkel et al. (2003) can vary depending on the individual and the circumstances surrounding the breakup. For example, someone who is breaking up with a partner because they are moving away may have different face threats than someone who is breaking up because of infidelity.

Regardless of the specific face threats, it's common for both parties involved in a breakup to experience a sense of loss and a questioning of their identity. This can lead to feelings of sadness, anger, and confusion. It's important to acknowledge these feelings and allow yourself to grieve the loss of the relationship. This can involve talking to friends or family, seeking professional counselling, or engaging in self-care activities such as exercise or meditation.

It's also important to remember that healing from a breakup takes time and that there is no "right" way to go through the process. It's normal to have ups and downs, and to experience setbacks along the way.

Ultimately, the key to healing from a breakup is to focus on self-growth and self-love. This can involve setting goals for the future, pursuing hobbies and interests, and practicing self-compassion. With time and effort, it is possible to move on from a breakup and emerge stronger and more resilient than before.

Navigating the Five Stages of the Breakup Model: Understanding the Process of Ending a Relationship.

Breaking up with a significant other is never easy, and there is no one-size-fits-all approach that will work for every relationship. This is precisely why numerous studies have been conducted to determine the best way to break up with someone. The Duck breakup model, created by Steve Duck in 1982 and updated in 2005, recognizes that relationships are contextual and will vary from person to person, making it difficult to determine a single "best way" to end a relationship.

The breakup model can be broken down into five stages: intrapsychic processes, dyadic processes, social processes, grave-dressing processes, and resurrection processes.

1. Intrapsychic Processes: The first stage of the breakup model involves one partner feeling burdened with resentment and no longer benefitting from the relationship. This can happen due to a variety of reasons, such as growing apart, lack of compatibility, or betrayal. This stage involves the partner experiencing emotional turmoil as they come to terms with their unhappiness in the relationship. They may start to withdraw socially from their partner and others who they typically associate with.

2. Dyadic Processes: The second stage involves the partner who is experiencing unhappiness disclosing their feelings to their

significant other. This step is essential because it allows the potential for the relationship to ultimately end or improve. It is essential that the partner communicates their feelings in an open and honest manner, without blaming or attacking their partner. A resolution must occur between both partners with proper communication methods.

3. Social Processes: The third stage involves word of the distress of the relationship being made known to those outside of the relationship. This stage can make it difficult to step back and fix the problem(s) because opinions and judgments of others may influence the decision-making process of both partners.

4. Grave-Dressing Processes: Once the relationship is over, the fourth stage involves individuals processing the breakup and beginning to move on. It's normal for individuals to speak negatively about their ex-partner to others and start the process of letting go. This stage involves individuals processing the emotions and memories associated with the relationship and starting to make sense of what happened. It's important to note that individuals may grieve the loss of the relationship during this stage.

5. Resurrection Processes: The final stage involves individuals reflecting on the actions of themselves and their ex-partner to determine potential changes for future relationships. This could include awareness of their own mistakes and how they will change for their next romance or traits they may want to avoid while searching for a partner. This stage involves a level of self-reflection and self-improvement as individuals prepare themselves for future relationships.

the breakup model offers a useful framework for understanding the stages individuals go through during a breakup. While every breakup is unique, understanding these stages can help individuals navigate the process and move towards healing and growth.

While there is no "best way" to break up with someone, Duck recommends that the most important aspect of the breakup model is to be prepared. Being prepared means having the knowledge to intervene or change one's behaviour before it is too late. By recognizing the stages of the breakup model, individuals can have a better understanding of the process of ending a relationship and can be better prepared to handle it emotionally.

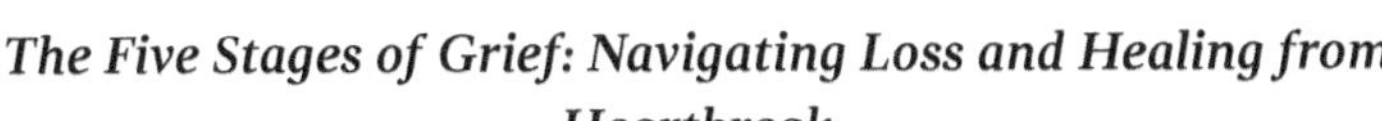

The Five Stages of Grief: Navigating Loss and Healing from Heartbreak

Breakups can be a difficult and painful experience, and it is natural to feel a wide range of emotions during this time. One common way of understanding the process of healing from heartbreak is through the five stages of grief, as outlined by psychiatrist Elisabeth Kubler-Ross in her book "On Death and Dying." While these stages were initially meant to describe the process of coping with death, they can also be applied to other forms of loss, including the end of a relationship. In this chapter, we will explore each of these five stages in depth, and provide tips and strategies for navigating through them.

1. Denial:

The first stage of grief is denial, which is characterized by a sense of disbelief and shock. During this stage, individuals may struggle to accept the reality of the loss, and may instead cling to a sense of hope that things will somehow return to how they were before. It is important to recognize that denial is a natural response to loss, but it is also important to gradually accept the reality of the situation and begin the process of healing.

1. Anger:

The second stage of grief is anger, which is often characterized by feelings of frustration, irritation, and resentment. The individual may feel that they have been unfairly treated or that they have been robbed of something that was rightfully theirs. They may lash out at others or feel a sense of intense frustration and anger towards themselves. It is important to find healthy ways to express and process anger, such as through exercise, journaling, or talking to a trusted friend or therapist.

3. Bargaining:

The third stage of grief is bargaining, which is characterized by a sense of bargaining or negotiation with a higher power or with others. The individual may try to make deals or promises in order to try to reverse the loss or avoid future losses. While it is natural to try to find solutions or ways to avoid pain, it is important to recognize that some losses are inevitable and that bargaining may not be a productive coping strategy in the long run.

4. Depression:

The fourth stage of grief is depression, which is characterized by feelings of sadness, despair, and hopelessness. The individual may feel overwhelmed by the loss and may struggle to find any sense of meaning or purpose in life. They may experience physical symptoms such as fatigue, insomnia, or changes in appetite. It is important to seek support during this stage, whether through therapy, support groups, or connecting with loved ones.

5. Acceptance:

The final stage of grief is acceptance, which is characterized by a sense of peace and resolution. The individual has come to terms with the reality of the loss and has accepted that it is a part of their life. While they may still feel sadness or pain, they are able to move forward and find new meaning and purpose in life. It is important to note that acceptance does not necessarily mean that the individual is completely over their loss, but rather that they have found a way to live with it and move forward.

The process of healing from heartbreak is not always easy, but by understanding the five stages of grief, individuals can gain insight into their emotions and find ways to cope and move forward. It is important to be patient and kind to oneself during this time, and to seek support when needed. Ultimately, healing from heartbreak is a journey, but by taking it one step at a time, individuals can find their way to a place of acceptance and healing.

The Art of Breaking Up: How to End a Relationship with Respect and Empathy

Breaking up with someone can be a difficult and emotional experience, but it's important to do it in a way that is respectful and empathetic to the other person's feelings. Ghosting, or ending a relationship by simply disappearing, can be hurtful and damaging to both parties involved. Instead, there are guidelines that can be followed to have an ideal breakup.

The Ten "Rules":

1. Always break up in person and, if possible, not in public. Breaking up in person is considered the most respectful way to end a relationship, as it shows that you value the other person enough to have a face-to-face conversation. It's also best to choose a private location where you can talk without interruptions.

2. Avoid making a scene and control your emotions. While it's understandable to feel emotional during a breakup, it's important to avoid making a scene or saying hurtful things in the heat of the moment. Take deep breaths and try to remain as calm and composed as possible.

3. Do not feel as if you have to make the other person feel better. While it's natural to want to comfort the other person, it's not your responsibility to make them feel better. Trying to do so can lead to mixed signals and false hope, which can make the

breakup more difficult for both parties in the long run.

4. After the breakup, cut all contact until everything has settled. This can be one of the hardest rules to follow, but it's important to give both yourself and the other person space and time to process the breakup. Continuing to communicate can prolong the healing process and make it harder to move on.

5. Talk about it to those you are close to. Bottling up your emotions after a breakup can be harmful to your mental health, so it's important to talk to trusted friends or family members. Sharing your feelings can help you process the breakup and gain valuable support.

6. You can be sad, angry, or upset, but don't blame just one person or thing. It's natural to feel a range of emotions after a breakup, but it's important not to place blame solely on one person or thing. Relationships are a two-way street, and it's likely that both parties contributed to the breakup in some way.

7. Recognize that the relationship did not work and that you are both better off apart. It's important to come to terms with the fact that the relationship didn't work out, and that it's ultimately better for both parties to move on. Holding onto false hope can make the healing process more difficult.

8. Re-discover who you are as an individual. After a breakup, it can be helpful to take time for self-reflection and rediscovery. Take up new hobbies, spend time with friends, and focus on personal growth.

9. Do not start dating again until you are truly ready. While rebound relationships can be tempting, it's important to give yourself time to heal and process the breakup before jumping into a new relationship. Rushing into a new relationship can lead to unresolved emotional baggage and can hinder your ability to form a healthy relationship.

10. Only attempt to be friends with your ex-partner if you are both over the idea of dating. Attempting to remain friends with an ex-partner can be difficult, particularly if one or both parties still have romantic feelings. If you do decide to remain friends, it's

important to be honest about your intentions and to set clear boundaries.

The Importance of Empathy:

It's important to remember that the person you're breaking up with has feelings and emotions too. Being empathetic towards them and trying to understand their perspective can make the breakup process less painful for both parties involved. Taking into consideration the personal history between both partners and being respectful of their feelings can make a significant difference in the outcome of the breakup.

Following a breakup, it's essential to take care of oneself and allow for a grieving period. Re-discovering oneself and finding new meaning and purpose in life can help with the healing process. It's important to remember that everyone grieves differently and that there is no set timeline for moving on.

Breaking up with someone is never easy, but doing it with respect and empathy can make a significant difference in the aftermath. By following these guidelines and being mindful of the other person's feelings, it's possible to end a relationship in a way that is less painful for both parties involved.

CHAPTER THIRTEEN

BREAKING UP: COPING MECHANISMS AND GENDER DIFFERENCES

When a relationship comes to an end, it is often because the two parties involved want different things out of life. This can be a difficult realization to come to, and it can be especially challenging when the couple is not on the same page about the future of their relationship. In these situations, coping with the breakup can be very different for men and women.

When a relationship ends, it can be a difficult and emotional time for both parties involved. However, men and women may have different ways of coping with the aftermath of a breakup.

Men may often try to distract themselves from their feelings by keeping themselves busy with work or hobbies. They may also try to move on quickly by seeking out new relationships. On the other hand, women may be more inclined to process their emotions directly, seeking support from friends and family, and taking time to reflect on the relationship and what they want in the future.

While these are generalizations, understanding the gender differences in coping mechanisms can be helpful in navigating the aftermath of a breakup. It is important to allow yourself to feel your emotions and to process them in a healthy way, regardless of gender. Healing from a breakup takes time and self-compassion, and it's important to take care of yourself during this period.

Men and women often have different coping mechanisms when dealing with the end of a relationship. Men may be more likely to try to distract themselves from their feelings, whether it be through work, hobbies, or other activities. They may also try to move on quickly, often by seeking out new relationships. This can be a way for men to avoid dealing with the pain of the breakup and to feel like they are still in control of their lives.

Women, on the other hand, may be more likely to process their feelings and emotions directly. They may seek out support from friends and family, or they may turn to therapy or counselling to help them work through their grief. Women may also take time to reflect on the relationship and to understand what they want and need in a partner moving forward. This can be a more introspective approach to coping with a breakup, but it can also be more effective in the long run.

Of course, these are generalizations, and there are plenty of men who take a more introspective approach to coping with a breakup, and there are plenty of women who try to distract themselves from their feelings. However, understanding these differences in coping mechanisms can be helpful in navigating the aftermath of a breakup.

Regardless of gender, it is important to remember that healing from a breakup takes time. It is normal to feel a range of emotions, including sadness, anger, and confusion. It is also important to take care of yourself during this time, whether it be by practicing self-care, seeking out support from loved ones, or pursuing new hobbies or interests.

Ultimately, the key to coping with a breakup is to allow yourself to feel your emotions and to process them in a healthy way.

Whether you are a man or a woman, the road to healing may be long and challenging, but with time, patience, and self-compassion, it is possible to move on and find happiness once again.

Healing After Heartbreak: Understanding How Men and Women Cope Differently

It is important to acknowledge that men and women often have different ways of processing information, including how they cope with breakups. Research has shown that women tend to be more selective when choosing a partner, as they often plan for the long-term and look for qualities that would make someone a good candidate for raising a family. This can lead to women being more subject to rejection, as they may hold higher standards for their partners. Men, on the other hand, tend to be less selective and may face heavier costs if a long-term relationship ends.

A study by Choo et al. (1996) found that men and women have different emotional reactions to breakups. Men reported feeling less joy and relief after a breakup compared to women, but both genders reported similar levels of sadness, anger, guilt, and anxiety. Women were more likely to blame their partner for the problems in the relationship, while men tended to distract themselves with work or sports following the breakup.

It is important to note that these are generalizations and that each individual will have their own unique way of coping with a breakup, regardless of their gender. As an author writing about healing from heartbreak, it is important to approach the topic with empathy and understanding for the diverse ways that people experience and cope with the end of a relationship.

In addition to the aforementioned differences in coping mechanisms between men and women, research has also found that men are more likely to engage in rebound relationships following a breakup. This may be because men are more likely to view sex as a means of coping with emotional distress, while women tend to view it as a means of expressing intimacy and commitment

Furthermore, men and women may also differ in their willingness to seek professional help for dealing with the aftermath of a breakup. While women are more likely to seek out therapy or counselling, men may be more hesitant to do so, which can prolong their healing process and lead to long-term emotional distress

In light of these findings, it is important for individuals of all genders to prioritize their mental health and seek support when needed. This may involve seeking out therapy or counselling, talking to trusted friends or family members, or engaging in self-care activities such as exercise or mindfulness practices.

How Men and Women Cope with Breakups: Exploring Gender Differences and Similarities

The study conducted by Perilloux and Buss (2008) aimed to investigate the differences between male and female reactions to romantic breakups in greater detail. The study involved 98 males and 101 females who were asked to answer a series of questions related to their previous breakups, including the emotions they experienced, the costs of the breakup, and any strategies they used to cope with the breakup.

One key finding from the study was that men were more successful than women at preventing a breakup by increasing their level of commitment. This suggests that men may be more willing to work on their relationships and make an effort to keep them going.

Additionally, the study found that males who planned on ending their relationship were more likely to have intercourse with another individual before the breakup occurred than females. This may be because men are more likely to view sex as a means of coping with emotional distress, as mentioned earlier.

Another interesting finding was that women who were broken up with reported feeling sad or confused, while men may feel happy or indifferent. This could be because women may invest more time and emotional energy into their relationships, making the loss of the relationship more impactful for them.

Finally, the study found that women reported higher costs, including stalking or loss of protection after breaking up with their partner. This highlights the potential dangers that women may face when ending a relationship, and the importance of seeking out support and protection if necessary.

Overall, both studies suggest that men and women tend to process breakups differently, with women being more emotionally expressive and men being more likely to ignore or suppress their emotions. However, it is important to remember that these are general trends, and individuals of all genders may react to breakups in unique ways.

The Perils of Post-Breakup Violence: Understanding the Risks of Ending a Relationship with an Unstable Partner

The end of a romantic relationship can be a difficult and emotional time for both parties involved. However, for some individuals, particularly those who are emotionally unstable, the end of a relationship can trigger violent and even deadly behaviour. This is especially true for the person who is left or dumped in the relationship, known as the "dumpee". The period after a breakup is when the true danger of ending a relationship can occur.

Stalking, assault, and even murder are some of the serious risks associated with breaking up with an unstable partner. In a 2011 survey, it was found that around 50% of stalking cases were carried out by a partner or ex-partner, and of these cases, 62% involved female victims (Logan, 2011). This indicates that women are particularly vulnerable to post-breakup violence and stalking.

Statistically, men are more likely to be the aggressors in cases of post-breakup violence, especially in cases of sexual assault and domestic abuse. Stalking is a common precursor to more violent crimes and can continue for a long period, with an average duration of 1-2.2 years. The stalking behaviour can include physical surveillance, unwanted phone calls, property invasion/damage, or proxy stalking (Logan, 2012). As time goes on, the obsession with the ex-partner can build, eventually leading to violent behaviour.

It is important for endangered individuals to involve law enforcement immediately when such behaviour arises. While men are statistically more likely to react in violence following a breakup, it is important to remember that ex-partner crimes occur every day with both female and male victims. In addition, the duration of the relationship and age can also be factors in the likelihood of post-breakup violence. Adolescents and young adults have higher rates of victimization than older individuals, particularly females in long-term relationships.

In conclusion, ending a relationship can be a challenging time for everyone involved, and for some individuals, it can trigger violent and even deadly behaviour. Stalking, assault, and murder are some of the deadly risks of breaking up with an emotionally unstable partner. It is important for endangered individuals to involve law enforcement immediately when such behaviour arises.

CHAPTER FOURTEEN

MOVING FORWARD AFTER HEARTBREAK

"*"Letting go means to come to the realization that some people are a part of your history, but not a part of your destiny." –Steve Maraboli*"

In this chapter, we will explore strategies for moving forward after experiencing heartbreak. We will discuss how to let go of the past and create a new future for ourselves.

After experiencing heartbreak, it can be difficult to move on and start a new chapter in our lives. We may feel stuck in the past, unable to let go of the hurt and pain we have experienced. However, it is important to remember that healing is a process and that moving forward is possible.

One strategy for moving forward is to focus on self-care. This can involve taking care of our physical and emotional health, engaging in activities that bring us joy and fulfilment, and surrounding ourselves with positive influences.

Another strategy is to practice forgiveness, both towards ourselves and others. Holding onto anger and resentment only prolongs the healing process and prevents us from moving forward. By letting go of negative emotions and practicing forgiveness, we can create space for healing and growth.

One important aspect of moving forward is to allow ourselves to feel the pain and sadness associated with heartbreak. It can be tempting to suppress these emotions or try to numb them with distractions, but it is important to acknowledge and process them in a healthy way. This may involve journaling, talking with a trusted friend or therapist, or engaging in creative activities like art or music.

Another important strategy is to focus on personal growth and development. This can involve setting new goals for ourselves, whether they be related to career, education, or personal relationships. It may also involve exploring new hobbies and interests or taking steps to improve our physical and mental health.

It is also important to surround ourselves with positive and supportive people. This may involve spending time with friends and family who lift us up and encourage us, or joining a support group for people who have experienced heartbreak or loss. By focusing on the future and creating a vision for ourselves, we can begin to move forward and create a new life after heartbreak.

Ultimately, moving forward after heartbreak requires patience, self-compassion, and a willingness to let go of the past. By embracing these strategies and committing to our own healing and growth, we can create a bright and fulfilling future for ourselves.

Finally, it is important to remember that healing is not a linear process. There may be setbacks and difficult days, but with time and self-compassion, we can continue to move forward and create a fulfilling life for ourselves after heartbreak.

CHAPTER FIFTEEN

TIME AS A TOOL FOR HEALING: MOVING FORWARD FROM HEARTBREAK

"Time heals what reason cannot." ~SENECA

It can be difficult to go through the pain and emotional turmoil of a breakup. It's a natural instinct to want to avoid the pain and find comfort in a new relationship. However, it's important to take the time to heal before jumping into a new relationship.

Taking time to heal after a breakup is not just about dealing with the pain and hurt, but also about understanding what went wrong in the previous relationship and what you want and need in a future relationship. It's an opportunity to learn from the past and make sure that the next relationship is more fulfilling and healthy.

Time can play a crucial role in the healing process of a broken relationship. In fact, the concept of time as a healer is a common one, and for good reason. Time can help to ease the pain and emotional distress of a breakup, and can also provide a perspective that is difficult to gain in the immediate aftermath of a relationship ending.

Time can be a helpful component of the healing process, it's important to also actively engage in the work of healing. In my book, I provide practical strategies and advice for how to do this, so that readers can feel empowered to take control of their own healing journey and move forward in a positive and healthy way.

There is no set timeline for healing from a heartbreak. Everyone's healing process is unique and varies depending on the individual's circumstances, mind-set, and support system. Healing can take weeks, months, or even years. It's important to be patient with yourself and allow yourself to go through the healing process at your own pace.

Healing from heartbreak is a journey, and it requires effort, intention, and support. It's not something that can be achieved overnight, but it's a process that can lead to growth and personal development. Seeking support from friends, family, or a therapist can be helpful in the healing process.

I believe that time can play a significant role in the healing process. When you experience heartbreak, it can feel like the pain and sadness will never go away. But as time passes, you may start to notice that the intensity of those feelings lessens.

One of the reasons that time can help heal heartbreak is that it allows for a natural process of emotional processing and adjustment to take place. After a breakup, it's common to experience intense emotions such as grief, anger, and sadness. These emotions can be overwhelming and make it difficult to think clearly or make good decisions. However, as time passes, these emotions may begin to subside, allowing you to gain a clearer perspective on the situation.

Another way that time can help with healing from heartbreak is by providing distance from the situation. When you're in the midst of a breakup, it can be hard to see beyond the pain and hurt that you're feeling. But as time goes by, you may find that you're able to view the situation with a more objective eye. This can allow you to see what went wrong in the relationship and to gain insights that can help you avoid similar problems in the future.

It's important to note, however, that time alone is not enough to heal from heartbreak. It's also important to actively work on the healing process by engaging in activities that promote emotional well-being and personal growth. This might include seeking support from friends or a therapist, practicing self-care, and pursuing interests or hobbies that bring you joy and fulfilment.

In addition to providing distance from the situation and allowing for emotional processing and adjustment, time can also provide an opportunity for personal growth and self-reflection. After a breakup, it's common to feel lost or unsure about who you are or what you want out of life. Taking the time to explore your interests, pursue new hobbies, or reflect on your values and goals can help you gain a sense of clarity and purpose.

Additionally, time can allow you to work through any lingering feelings of resentment or anger that you may be holding onto. When you're in the midst of a breakup, it can be difficult to see beyond the hurt and pain that you're feeling. But as time passes, you may find that you're able to forgive yourself and your ex-partner for any mistakes that were made, and to let go of any negative emotions that are holding you back.

It's important to note, however, that the amount of time it takes to heal from heartbreak can vary from person to person. While some people may start to feel better after a few weeks or months, others may take longer to fully process and move on from the breakup. It's important to honour your own unique healing journey and to not compare yourself to others.

While time can be a powerful tool in healing from heartbreak, it's important to actively engage in the healing process and to be patient and compassionate with yourself along the way. With time, support, and self-care, it is possible to move forward from heartbreak and find happiness and fulfilment in the future.

I'M NOT RIGHT FOR YOU THE AFTERMATH:

The aftermath of a breakup can be a difficult and emotionally challenging time for both partners. However, it is crucial for both individuals to accept the end of the relationship and begin the healing process in a healthy way. Duck's (2008) breakup model suggests that the "grave-dressing process" is an important part of healthy coping, which involves processing why the relationship ended in order to move on from it.

It is important that neither partner engages in behaviours that aim to hurt the other person or seek revenge. Rushing into a new relationship, pulling pranks, or threatening physical harm or violence are unhealthy ways to cope with the breakup and will only lead to more hurt and pain. Instead, both individuals should desire to move past the heartache by coping in healthy ways.

20 healthy coping methods after a breakup:

1. Embrace your feelings: Allow yourself to feel and process your emotions, whether it be sadness, anger, or frustration. Avoid suppressing your emotions, as it can hinder the healing process.

2. Be willing to openly discuss your emotions: Find a trusted friend or family member to talk to about your emotions. It can be helpful to express how you are feeling and receive validation and support.

3. Write down how you are feeling: Writing down your emotions in a journal or diary can help you reflect on your feelings and track your progress as you heal.

4. Understand that breakups are, at times, inevitable: Recognize that relationships can end for various reasons, and it is not always within your control. Accepting this fact can help you move on.

5. Do not take the loss personally: Avoid blaming yourself for the breakup or thinking that you are not good enough. Remember that relationships require effort from both parties, and the end of a relationship does not define your self-worth.

6. Prioritize your needs and emotions: Focus on taking care of yourself and your emotional well-being during this time.

7. Develop or rediscover a routine: Establishing a routine can provide a sense of stability and normalcy during a time of uncertainty and change.

8. Take time to yourself and remember to pamper yourself: Treat yourself to activities that make you happy and relaxed, such as reading a book, taking a bath, or getting a massage.

9. Give yourself some slack: Avoid putting pressure on yourself to move on quickly or have everything figured out. Healing takes time, and it is okay to take things at your own pace.

10. Maintain your faith in others and relationships: Remember that not all relationships are the same and that there are good people out there.

11. Let go of hope for getting back together with your partner: Accepting that the relationship has ended and that there is no hope of reconciliation can help you move forward.

12. Do not attempt to maintain a friendship with your ex: It can be challenging to move on when you continue to have contact with your ex-partner. Avoid attempting to maintain a friendship until

you have healed and are ready.

13. Avoid unhealthy people or coping strategies: Surround yourself with positive and supportive people, and avoid unhealthy coping strategies such as substance abuse or self-harm.

14. Keep a list of your ex-partner's worst qualities: It can be helpful to remind yourself of the reasons why the relationship ended and the negative qualities of your ex-partner.

15. Do not attempt to get revenge: Avoid seeking revenge on your ex-partner, as it will not help you heal and can potentially harm yourself or others.

16. Learn from the failed relationship: Reflect on what went wrong in the relationship and identify areas where you can improve for future relationships.

17. Remember the benefits of being single: Focus on the positives of being single, such as the freedom to pursue personal goals and hobbies.

18. Get closure for yourself, by yourself: Closure does not always come from the other person. Find closure within yourself by accepting the end of the relationship and moving forward.

19. Do not forget that you can survive by yourself: Remember that you are strong and capable of handling life on your own.

20. Start dating again when you are ready: Take your time and only start dating again when you feel ready and have fully healed from the previous relationship.

By following these healthy coping strategies, individuals can move on from the pain and heartache of a breakup and start a new chapter in their lives. It is important to remember that the healing process takes time, and it is crucial to be patient with yourself as you work through your emotions and move forward.

Understanding the Complexity of On-Off Relationships: The Consequences of Not Coping with Breakups Properly

the aftermath of a breakup can be emotionally challenging for many individuals, particularly for those who have difficulty letting go of a past relationship. Excessive rumination is a common problem that many people face after a breakup, and it can be challenging to move past this issue without receiving an explanation for the relationship's dissolution. If a breakup is not properly coped with, it can lead to feelings of unsettledness, depression, psychological distress, and reduced life satisfaction. This can impact an individual's well-being and overall perception of romantic relationships.

For some people, walking away from a past relationship can be challenging, especially if both partners choose to stay in contact after the breakup. This can be particularly problematic if the relationship continues in a seemingly platonic manner, and individuals begin to view their ex-partner through rose-coloured glasses

One partner may promise to change their previous habits or otherwise resolve past conflicts that caused the breakup, which can convince the other person that there is potential for the relationship to grow stronger or return to a previous state. However, old habits are challenging to break, and many couples who break up once due to past behaviours and get back together before the coping process has completed enter an on-again/off-again relationship. Each time a breakup occurs, there is a natural expectation for the couple to renegotiate or redefine the terms of the relationship to avoid breaking up again, creating a continually evolving agreement of the relationship terms. While this can allow both partners to express their needs and adhere to the other individual's requests, it often leads to problems with communication, which is one of the largest indicators of a breakup, according to research.

Although on-again/off-again partners report lower relational quality, factors such as lingering feelings, developing better communication skills, negative experiences with other relationships, and visible changes in the partners or the relationship continue to drive couples to continue renewing the relationship. The problem with on-off relationships is that they often do not allow the time and space required after a breakup to cope, heal, and come to terms with why the relationship failed and what is required of each partner to adjust before making another attempt at a partnership. To avoid the continuous heartbreak and emotional exhaustion that an on-off relationship causes, it is essential to give the other person space, cut all ties of communication, grow as separate individuals, learn from past mistakes, and when both partners feel ready, maybe it is time to try again. However, it is essential to remember that not every relationship is meant to be long-term, which is perfectly normal.

In addition to on-and-off again relationships, some individuals may struggle to let go of a past relationship even if it was a relatively short-lived one. This is often due to the intense emotional connection and attachment that they formed with their partner, making it difficult for them to move on and start anew.

Some individuals may also hold onto the idea of their ex-partner, projecting an idealized version of them onto their memories and refusing to acknowledge any negative aspects of the relationship. This can lead to a skewed perception of the past and hinder the individual's ability to move forward and find closure.

Another factor that may contribute to difficulty in letting go of a past relationship is a fear of being alone or starting over. This can be particularly true for individuals who have invested a significant amount of time and effort into the relationship, or for those who may feel that their options for finding a new partner are limited.

Despite these challenges, it is important for individuals to recognize the value in letting go of a past relationship and moving on. This can involve acknowledging and processing their emotions, focusing on self-care and personal growth, and seeking support from friends, family, or a therapist. By letting go of the past, individuals can open themselves up to new opportunities and experiences, ultimately leading to a happier and more fulfilling life.

The Three Stages of Romantic Relationships: Understanding Compatibility and Growth

The idea that just because a relationship ends doesn't mean it has failed is an important one to consider. The concept of the three stages of romantic relationships is also valuable in understanding how relationships develop and change over time. The first stage of romantic love is characterized by passion, attraction, and excitement. However, as couples progress into the second stage, they may experience challenges such as distractions, arguments, and a loss of romance. Many couples who are unable to navigate these challenges end their relationship at this stage.

1. Romantic love: This stage is characterized by high levels of passion, intimacy, and attraction. Couples in this stage often feel like they are on cloud nine, and everything seems perfect. They tend to idealize their partner and overlook any flaws or issues in the relationship. This stage can last anywhere from a few months to a couple of years, depending on the couple.

2. Discouragement and distraction: As the relationship progresses, couples often experience a shift in their emotions and attitudes towards each other. This stage is marked by a decline in the intensity of passion and romance, and couples may start to feel disillusioned. Distractions like work, school, or family obligations can also take a toll on the relationship, leading to feelings of neglect or dissatisfaction. This is often the stage where couples start to argue and fight more frequently.

3. Separation, adjustment with resignation, or adjustment with contentment: This final stage can go one of three ways. Couples may choose to end the relationship if they cannot resolve their differences or if they feel like they have grown too far apart. Alternatively, they may decide to stay together out of resignation, feeling like they have invested too much time and effort into the relationship to just give up. This approach often leads to an unhappy relationship marked by feelings of resentment or regret. Finally, couples may choose to work on their relationship and adjust their expectations to create a new normal. This approach leads to a happy and fulfilling partnership

based on mutual respect, trust, and love.

Understanding the three stages of romantic relationships can help individuals navigate the challenges they may face in their partnership. While every relationship is unique, these stages provide a useful framework for understanding the ebb and flow of emotions and attitudes that couples may experience. Remember, just because a relationship ends doesn't mean it has failed. With patience, communication, and a willingness to work through issues, couples can create a happy and long-lasting partnership.

Understanding the three stages of romantic relationships can help couples better navigate the ups and downs of their partnership. Instead of seeing the end of a relationship as a failure, it can be viewed as a natural part of the development and growth of two individuals. By recognizing the challenges of the second stage and finding healthy ways to work through them, couples may be able to build a stronger and more enduring connection.

In addition to understanding the three stages of romantic relationships, it is also important to recognize that compatibility can change over time as individuals grow and develop. This does not necessarily mean that the relationship has failed or that there is anything inherently wrong with either partner. Rather, it may simply be a natural evolution of the relationship as each person goes through different life experiences.

Furthermore, it is important to note that healthy communication is key to navigating the ups and downs of any relationship. Couples who are able to openly discuss their feelings, concerns, and needs with each other are more likely to be able to work through the challenges that arise in the second stage of the relationship and move on to a happier and more fulfilling partnership in the third stage.

It is also worth noting that not all relationships will make it through all three stages, and that is okay. Sometimes, two people may simply not be compatible in the long-term, or they may have different goals and aspirations that lead them in different directions. In these cases, it is important to recognize when it is time to move on and to do so in a respectful and healthy manner.

Understanding the three stages of romantic relationships can help individuals navigate the ups and downs of their partnerships and recognize when it is time to move on. By focusing on healthy communication, personal growth, and mutual respect, couples can build strong, fulfilling relationships that stand the test of time.

The Breakup Process: Understanding and Coping with the End of a Relationship

Breaking up with someone can be a challenging experience, but it can also be an opportunity for growth and self-discovery. It is crucial to be prepared for the breakup process, regardless of whether you are the one initiating the breakup or being broken up with. Those who are being broken up with may need guidance on how to cope with the loss of a partnership and move on.

The intrapsychic process of the breakup model is the first stage, where the dumper begins to feel dissatisfied with the terms or events of the relationship. They may feel obliged to disclose their resentment to their partner, which is one of the predictors of an upcoming breakup. The dumpee is responsible for identifying their partner's dissatisfied needs and renegotiating the terms of the relationship so that they are no longer unfulfilled.

If the issues threatening the relationship are not resolved, the breakup goes into the dyadic phase of the breakup model. The dumper continues to feel unhappy, while the dumpee seemingly ignores their needs. If this dissatisfaction is left unresolved, it may lead to a breakup, and people outside of the relationship are made aware of the impending breakup.

However, ending a relationship carries risks, such as depression, sleep disturbances, intrusive thoughts, broken heart syndrome, endocrine and immunity dysfunctions, and partner violence. Partner violence is a severe risk that can victimize both men and women.

The final stage of the breakup process is grave-dressing, where both partners decide what went wrong on both sides of the relationship. It marks the beginning of the healing process and can help both partners gain closure and move on. It is essential to recognize that breaking up can be a challenging and painful experience, but with time and self-reflection, it can also lead to personal growth and emotional healing.

After the grave-dressing phase, individuals may go through a resurrection process in which they rediscover themselves and start rebuilding their lives. This is a time for self-reflection and personal growth, and it can lead to positive changes in their lives.

During this time, it's important to focus on self-care and take care of one's physical and mental health. Activities such as exercise, meditation, and spending time with friends and family can help individuals heal and move on from the breakup.

It's also important to acknowledge and process the emotions that come with a breakup, such as anger, sadness, and loneliness. Talking to a therapist or counsellor can be helpful in managing these emotions and navigating the healing process.

Finally, it's important to remember that healing from a breakup is a process that takes time. There may be setbacks and challenges along the way, but with patience and self-compassion, individuals can emerge stronger and more resilient than before.

Breakups are a complex and unique experience that can vary greatly between couples, and there is no one perfect way to end a relationship. However, research has shed light on some helpful tips and insights into the breakup process. One significant factor is age, as younger generations tend to prefer online breakups, while older generations may prefer in-person communication.

The most ideal way to end a relationship involves avoiding a scene, cutting all contact with one another, healing independently, and refraining from starting new relationships until the coping process is completed. It's essential to take time to heal and not rush into another relationship too quickly, as compatibility can fluctuate over time.

Men and women tend to cope differently with breakups. Women tend to be more selective in their partnerships and may feel joy or relief more often than men following a breakup. Men, on the other hand, may distract themselves with work or sports and feel happy or indifferent after a breakup. Women also tend to react emotionally and may blame their partner once it's over.

It's important to note that breakups do not equal failure, and it's natural for relationships to end. The three phases of romantic relationships include the initial honeymoon phase, discouragement as life's distractions arise, and the final make-or-break phase. Not every relationship is meant to be long-term, but couples should try healthier alternatives before ending the relationship.

The aftermath of a breakup can be challenging and lonely, but surrounding oneself with loved ones, rediscovering routines and enjoyments, and appreciating the single life while allowing time and space away from relationships can help with healing and concluding an ideal breakup.

Additionally, it's important to acknowledge that the aftermath of a breakup can also bring about positive growth and change. For example, it can provide an opportunity for self-reflection and a chance to re-evaluate one's values, goals, and priorities in life. It can also lead to newfound independence and a chance to pursue personal interests and hobbies that may have been neglected during the relationship.

Furthermore, it's important for individuals to take care of themselves during and after a breakup. This can include seeking support from friends and family, practicing self-care activities such as exercise or meditation, and seeking professional help if needed. It's also important to avoid unhealthy coping mechanisms such as substance abuse or rebound relationships.

While breakups can be difficult and painful, they are a natural part of relationships and can provide an opportunity for growth and positive change. Coping strategies and self-care are important during the aftermath of a breakup, and couples should consider healthier alternatives before ending a relationship.

CHAPTER EIGHTEEN

MENDING A BROKEN HEART: STRATEGIES FOR HEALING AND MOVING ON

"Everybody needs a hug. It changes your metabolism."
LEO BUSCAGLIA

Heartbreak is a painful experience that can leave us feeling lost and alone. The end of a relationship can be devastating, leaving us feeling hopeless and unsure of how to move forward. However, it is important to remember that healing from heartbreak is possible.

The journey to healing from heartbreak is different for everyone, but there are some common strategies that can help ease the pain and guide us towards a happier, more fulfilling future. In this chapter, we will explore some of these strategies and how they can be implemented in our daily lives.

Allowing Yourself to Grieve

The first step towards healing from heartbreak is to allow yourself to grieve. It is normal to feel a range of emotions, including sadness, anger, and confusion. Trying to suppress or ignore these emotions can prolong the healing process and prevent us from moving forward.

Instead, it is important to give yourself permission to feel and process these emotions in a healthy way. This might involve talking to a trusted friend or family member, writing in a journal, or seeking out professional support such as therapy or counselling.

Music as a Therapy

Music has been shown to have therapeutic effects on our emotions and can be a helpful tool in healing from heartbreak. Listening to music that speaks to our emotions can provide a sense of comfort and catharsis. It can also help us process our emotions and find meaning in our experiences.

Playing music or singing can also be a helpful form of self-expression and a way to connect with others who share similar experiences.

Socializing and Making New Connections

Socializing and making new connections can be a helpful way to distract ourselves from our pain and to find support and comfort from others. This might involve joining a social club or group, attending events or parties, or simply reaching out to friends or family members.

Making new connections can also help us broaden our perspectives and gain new insights into ourselves and our experiences. It can be a way to rediscover our sense of identity and purpose.

Exercise and Self-Care

Exercise and self-care are essential components of healing from heartbreak. Physical activity can help us release pent-up emotions and boost our mood. It can also improve our overall health and well-being, helping us feel more confident and empowered.

Self-care involves prioritizing our physical and emotional needs and taking steps to meet them. This might involve getting enough sleep, eating healthy foods, practicing relaxation techniques such as meditation or yoga, or engaging in hobbies and activities that bring us joy.

Overall, healing from heartbreak is a process that takes time and effort. It requires us to be patient, compassionate, and open to new experiences and perspectives. By implementing these strategies, we can navigate the journey towards healing and emerge stronger, more resilient, and more fulfilled than ever before.

Healing for Your Body

"The power of love to change bodies is legendary, built into folklore, common sense, and
everyday experience. Love moves the flesh; it pushes matter around.... Throughout history,
"tender loving care" has uniformly been recognized as a valuable element in healing. ~LARRY
DOSSE"

The quote by Larry Dossey highlights the power of love in healing our bodies. It is a well-known fact that love can influence our physical and mental health in numerous ways. Love can change our bodies and push matter around. It has a profound effect on our overall wellbeing. This is why "tender loving care" has been recognized as an essential element in healing throughout history.

As holistic beings, we are not just made up of flesh and bones, but also mind, soul, and spirit. Every aspect of our being affects everything else. Therefore, when we are going through a heartbreak, it is crucial to take care of our body, mind, soul, and spirit. This book aims to help readers heal their broken hearts by taking care of themselves in every aspect.

Everyone has their own ideas and beliefs about health. However, the main idea is to have an intention of supporting our body's overall health and making choices that align with that intention. We need to show our body how much we value and appreciate it. If the break-up was due to infidelity or exposure to sexually transmitted diseases, it is crucial to get a check-up right away.

It is also essential to have regular physical check-ups to send a positive message to our subconscious that we are proactive about caring for ourselves. Below is a list of actions we can take to support our body's overall health, and we can add our own ideas to this list as well. The actions can be different for each individual, such as eating extra protein or watching less TV, or eating more vegetarian food or relaxing enough to watch a bit of TV.

taking care of ourselves in every aspect is essential for healing our broken hearts. Love can have a powerful effect on our bodies, and by taking care of ourselves, we can facilitate the healing process. We need to find what works for us and start with one or two changes.

The power of love to heal and transform goes beyond just physical health. Love has the ability to heal emotional wounds and restore a wounded spirit. When we experience heartbreak, it can affect us on all levels of our being, including our emotional, mental, and spiritual health.

One of the ways to support emotional healing is through self-care practices such as meditation, yoga, journaling, or seeking therapy. These practices help us to process our emotions and release any negative energy that may be trapped within us. They also help us to cultivate a sense of inner peace and self-compassion, which can be instrumental in overcoming heartbreak.

In addition to self-care practices, it is also important to seek support from friends and family members. Talking to someone about your feelings and experiences can help to ease the pain and provide a sense of comfort and validation. This can also be a great opportunity to receive guidance and support from those who have gone through similar experiences.

Another aspect of healing from heartbreak is spiritual growth. This can involve exploring your beliefs and values, practicing gratitude and forgiveness, or connecting with a higher power or purpose. Engaging in spiritual practices can help to provide a sense of meaning and purpose, as well as a source of comfort and hope during difficult times.

Overall, healing from heartbreak is a holistic process that involves taking care of all aspects of our being - body, mind, soul, and spirit. By adopting healthy self-care practices, seeking support from loved ones, and engaging in spiritual growth, we can overcome heartbreak and emerge stronger, more resilient, and more capable of giving and receiving love

Healing for Your Soul & Mind

"To a mind that is still, the whole universe surrenders.
~CHUANG TZŬ

"If someone should ask me, 'What does the soul do?', I would say, 'It does two things. It loves.

And it creates. Those are its primary acts." ~SUE MONK KIDD"

Sue Monk Kidd's quote suggests that the soul has two primary acts: loving and creating. Love is a fundamental aspect of the human experience and has the power to transform our lives in many ways. Love allows us to connect with others on a deep level, form meaningful relationships, and experience the joy of giving and receiving. It is through love that we find purpose and meaning in life.

Creating is another essential aspect of the human experience. When we create, we express ourselves, explore our creativity, and find new ways to connect with the world around us. Whether it's through art, music, writing, or any other form of creative expression, creating allows us to tap into a deep well of inspiration and connect with our innermost selves.

When we experience a broken heart, our soul can be deeply affected. We may feel disconnected from ourselves, others, and the world around us. Our thoughts can become negative and self-defeating, and our energy can be drained. It's important to take steps to support our mind, our mental health, and our soul during this challenging time.

One way to support our mental health is to engage in activities that promote positive thinking and healthy habits. This might include reading uplifting books or listening to positive affirmations. It might also include practicing mindfulness or meditation, which can help calm our minds and reduce stress.

Engaging in creative activities is also a powerful way to support our soul during times of heartache. When we create, we tap into our innermost selves and express ourselves in new and meaningful ways. This can help us process our emotions and find new ways to connect with ourselves and others.

Ultimately, taking care of our mind, our mental health, and our soul is essential for healing a broken heart. By replacing negative thoughts with positive ones, engaging in creative activities, and practicing healthy habits, we can begin to heal and move forward with renewed hope and resilience.

Another important aspect of Sue Monk Kidd's quote is the idea that the soul is not a fixed or static entity, but rather a dynamic and evolving aspect of our being. Our experiences in life shape and mold our soul, and through love and creation, we can continue to grow and evolve as individuals.

In addition, the act of loving and creating can be a form of resistance against the negative forces in the world. When we choose to love and create, we are actively pushing back against hatred, fear, and division. By cultivating a spirit of love and creativity, we can make a positive impact on the world around us and create a better future for ourselves and others.

It's also important to recognize that the process of healing a broken heart is not linear or straightforward. It can be a complex and challenging journey, and it's okay to seek support and guidance from others along the way. Whether it's through therapy, support groups, or simply talking with trusted friends and family, reaching out for help can be an important step towards healing and growth.

it's worth noting that loving and creating are not mutually exclusive acts. In fact, they often go hand in hand. When we love, we create space for new connections and experiences. When we create, we infuse our work with love and passion, and this can be felt by others who engage with our creations. By embracing both love and creation, we can lead a more fulfilling and meaningful life, one that is full of joy, purpose, and connection.

Another way to support your mind and soul during a difficult time is to practice mindfulness and meditation. Mindfulness is the practice of being present in the moment, observing your thoughts and emotions without judgment. This can help you detach from the negative thoughts and emotions that are causing you pain and allow you to gain clarity and perspective.

Meditation is a form of mindfulness that involves focusing your attention on a specific object or mantra. This can help calm your mind and reduce stress and anxiety. You can find guided meditations online or through meditation apps, or you can simply sit quietly for a few minutes each day and focus on your breath.

Journaling can also be a helpful practice for processing your emotions and gaining insights into your thought patterns. Writing down your thoughts and feelings can help you identify patterns and triggers that may be contributing to your heartache, and it can also be a cathartic release for pent-up emotions.

Finally, it's important to remember that healing takes time and there is no "right" way to do it. Be patient and kind to yourself, and don't hesitate to seek support from friends, family, or a therapist if needed.

CHAPTER NINETEEN

THE ROAD TO HEALING: MUSIC, SOCIALIZING, AND EXERCISE AS THERAPIES FOR HEARTBREAK

The Road to Healing: Music, Socializing, and Exercise as Therapies for Heartbreak" is a book chapter that explores different ways of coping with heartbreak. This chapter discusses the therapeutic effects of music, socializing, and exercise on individuals who are going through a breakup.

The first section of the chapter focuses on the healing power of music. Music has been used for centuries as a way to express emotions and connect with others. Research shows that listening to music can have a positive impact on mood and can even reduce symptoms of depression and anxiety. The chapter delves into how different types of music can evoke different emotions and help individuals process their feelings.

The second section of the chapter explores the benefits of socializing. Going through a heartbreak can feel isolating, but connecting with others can be a powerful way to cope. The chapter discusses how joining clubs, meeting new people, and engaging in social activities can provide a sense of community and support during this difficult time. It also addresses how socializing can lead to new opportunities and perspectives, helping individuals move forward in their healing journey.

The final section of the chapter discusses the role of exercise in healing from heartbreak. Exercise has been shown to have numerous physical and mental health benefits, including reducing stress, improving mood, and increasing self-esteem. The chapter explores different types of exercise and how they can help individuals feel more confident and empowered as they navigate the healing process.

Overall, "The Road to Healing: Music, Socializing, and Exercise as Therapies for Heartbreak" emphasizes the importance of finding healthy ways to cope with heartbreak. By exploring different therapeutic approaches, individuals can discover the strategies that work best for them and ultimately find a path towards healing and happiness.

The Healing Power of Music

Music has been used for centuries to express emotion, tell stories, and bring people together. It is no wonder that it can also be used as a form of therapy to heal from heartbreak.

When we experience heartbreak, we often feel a range of intense emotions such as sadness, anger, and confusion. It can be difficult to process these feelings, and it may feel like there is no outlet for our pain. This is where music can be incredibly beneficial.

Listening to music can help us to connect with our emotions and provide a safe space to express them. Whether it is a song that perfectly captures our feelings or a melody that allows us to escape for a moment, music can be a powerful tool in the healing process.

But music therapy is more than just listening to songs. It can involve actively creating music, whether it be singing, playing an instrument, or even writing lyrics. Engaging in music in this way can help us to connect with our feelings on a deeper level and provide a sense of control over our emotions.

Music can also help us to feel connected to others who have experienced similar pain. When we listen to a song that speaks to our heartbreak, we can feel a sense of understanding and empathy from the artist and other listeners who have been through similar experiences. This can provide a sense of comfort and a reminder that we are not alone in our struggles.

Research has shown that music therapy can have a range of positive effects on mental health, including reducing anxiety and depression and improving overall mood. It can also provide a sense of empowerment and a renewed sense of purpose, as we engage in something that brings us joy and fulfilment.

Of course, music therapy is not a one-size-fits-all solution, and it may not work for everyone. It is important to find the types of music and activities that resonate with us personally and to engage in them in a way that feels comfortable and safe.

But for those who find solace in music, it can be a powerful tool in the healing process. Whether it is through listening, creating, or connecting with others, music can help us to process our emotions and find a path forward towards healing and happiness.

Music has a way of connecting with our emotions in a powerful way. It can stir up feelings of joy, sadness, nostalgia, and even heartbreak. For those going through a breakup, music can be a valuable tool in the healing process.

Listening to music can provide a sense of comfort and validation for those who are experiencing heartbreak. Hearing lyrics that reflect our own emotions and experiences can be a powerful reminder that we are not alone in our pain. In fact, many artists have written songs about heartbreak and the healing process, which can be incredibly relatable and cathartic for listeners.

Music can also provide a healthy outlet for expressing and processing our emotions. Singing or playing an instrument can be a way to release pent-up emotions and express ourselves in a creative way. For those who may not have the skills or desire to play an instrument, simply listening to music and singing along can also be a way to release tension and feel more grounded.

In addition to providing emotional support and a creative outlet, music can also have a physiological impact on the body. Research has shown that listening to music can lower stress levels and reduce symptoms of depression and anxiety. It can also have a positive effect on heart rate and blood pressure.

Some people may find it helpful to create a specific playlist of songs that resonate with their emotions and experiences. This playlist can be used as a tool for self-reflection and emotional processing. It can also be a source of comfort during difficult moments.

Overall, music can be a powerful tool for healing from heartbreak. Whether it's listening to songs that resonate with our emotions, playing an instrument, or simply singing along to our favourite tunes, music can provide comfort, validation, and a healthy outlet for expressing and processing our emotions.

The Healing Power of Socializing

When we're going through a heartbreak, it's common to feel isolated and alone. We may want to withdraw from the world and curl up in bed all day. While taking time to process our emotions is important, it's equally important to remember that socializing can be a powerful tool in healing from a heartbreak.

Clubbing, making new friends, and participating in other social activities can help us to regain a sense of normalcy and connect with others who can offer us support and encouragement.

Clubbing and Nightlife

One of the most popular ways to socialize and meet new people is by going out clubbing or to other nightlife events. These types of activities can be a great way to let loose, have fun, and meet new people who share similar interests.

If you're feeling anxious about going out alone, consider inviting a friend or two to join you. Alternatively, you could look for local events or meetups online, where you can connect with others who share your interests.

Making New Friends

*"Having afriend to listen to your problems and discuss
them with you is the beginning of finding a solution~Lao
Tzu"*

Another powerful way to socialize and heal from a heartbreak is by making new friends. When we're in a relationship, it's easy to become isolated from others and rely solely on our partner for support and companionship. However, making new friends can help us to expand our social circle and connect with others who can offer us fresh perspectives and new experiences.

To make new friends, consider joining a club or group that aligns with your interests, volunteering for a local organization, or taking a class or workshop. These types of activities can help you to meet others who share your passions and hobbies.

Other Social Activities

Finally, participating in other social activities can be a powerful way to heal from a heartbreak. This could include anything from attending a concert or festival, to participating in a sports league, to taking a cooking or dance class.

The key is to find activities that bring you joy and that allow you to connect with others in a positive way. By participating in these activities, you can begin to rebuild your confidence, connect with others who share your interests, and regain a sense of purpose and meaning in your life.

While socializing may not be the first thing that comes to mind when we think about healing from a heartbreak, it can be an incredibly powerful tool in our recovery. Clubbing, making new friends, and participating in other social activities can help us to regain a sense of normalcy, connect with others who can offer us support and encouragement, and begin to rebuild our confidence and sense of self. So don't be afraid to put yourself out there and try new things – you never know who you might meet or what new experiences you might have.

Medication and Exercise for Healing Heartbreak

Heartbreak can take a significant toll on our mental and physical well-being. It can cause sleeplessness, loss of appetite, and a general feeling of being unwell. When dealing with the aftermath of a breakup, it is essential to take care of ourselves, and one way to do that is through medication and exercise.

Medication

If you find that your emotions are overwhelming and difficult to manage, it may be worth talking to a mental health professional about the possibility of medication. Medication can help alleviate symptoms of depression, anxiety, and other mental health conditions that may arise as a result of heartbreak.

It is essential to remember that medication should be prescribed and taken under the guidance of a licensed medical professional. Additionally, it can take time for medication to take effect, so it is important to be patient and persistent with the process.

Exercise

Exercise is a powerful tool for healing from heartbreak. It can help improve our mood, reduce stress, and promote better sleep. When we exercise, our bodies release endorphins, which are natural mood boosters. This can help us feel better both physically and emotionally.

There are many different forms of exercise to choose from, and it is important to find an activity that you enjoy. It could be something as simple as taking a walk outside or something more intense like weightlifting or running. The important thing is to find an activity that you can commit to and that makes you feel good.

Exercise can also be a great way to meet new people and socialize. Joining a fitness class or sports team can help you make new friends and get involved in a community. This can be especially helpful if you are feeling isolated or lonely after a breakup.

Incorporating medication and exercise into your healing process can be a powerful way to take care of yourself after a heartbreak. By taking care of both your mental and physical health, you can help yourself move forward and find happiness once again.

CHAPTER TWENTY

WHAT NEXT?

"We can only be said to be alive in those moments when our hearts are conscious of us treasures. ~THORNTON WILDER"

When we experience a broken heart, we are forced to confront our deepest emotions and vulnerabilities. This process can be painful, but it also presents an opportunity for self-discovery and growth. By taking care of our body, mind, and spirit, we can begin to heal and gain clarity about what we truly want and need in life.

Through this process of self-reflection, we can begin to understand our own strengths and weaknesses, our patterns of behaviour, and our deepest desires. We may discover that we have been living in ways that are not true to ourselves, or that we have been seeking fulfilment in the wrong places.

As we gain clarity about our own needs and desires, we can begin to communicate more effectively with others, resolving conflicts and building stronger relationships. We can also start to create the life that we truly want for ourselves, rather than simply accepting the status quo.

Ultimately, this process can lead to a deep and lasting sense of peace, as we learn to empower ourselves and find fulfilment in our own lives. So while a broken heart may be painful in the moment, it can also be an incredible opportunity for growth and transformation.

There are some more thoughts on how a broken heart can be an opportunity for growth and self-discovery:

1. Improved self-awareness: Going through a difficult breakup can provide an opportunity to gain a deeper understanding of who you are and what you want in life. It can also help you recognize patterns and behaviours that may not be serving you well, and make positive changes accordingly.

2. Greater empathy: Experiencing heartbreak can increase your capacity for empathy and compassion towards others who may be going through similar challenges. It can also help you become more attuned to the emotional needs of those around you.

3. Increased resilience: Overcoming heartbreak can help you build resilience and emotional strength, as you learn to navigate difficult emotions and emerge stronger on the other side. This resilience can also serve you well in other areas of your life, such as in your career or personal relationships.

4. Finding new passions: The process of healing from a broken heart can also lead you to discover new passions and interests. Whether it's through trying out new hobbies or exploring different career paths, a broken heart can be the catalyst for positive change and growth in your life.

5. Deeper spiritual connection: Some people find that going through a difficult breakup can deepen their spiritual connection and sense of purpose in life. This may involve exploring new spiritual practices, connecting with a supportive community, or finding comfort in prayer or meditation.

CHAPTER TWENTY-ONE

EMBRACING A NEW BEGINNING

In this final chapter, we will explore the concept of embracing a new beginning after heartbreak. We will discuss how to let go of the past and create a bright and fulfilling future for ourselves.

Embracing a new beginning involves making a conscious choice to move forward and let go of the pain and hurt associated with heartbreak. It can be a difficult and scary process, but it is also an opportunity to create a fresh start and discover new possibilities.

One important aspect of embracing a new beginning is to focus on self-compassion and self-love. This means treating ourselves with kindness and understanding, and recognizing our own worth and value. It also involves letting go of self-blame and negative self-talk, and instead cultivating a positive and empowering inner dialogue.

Another key aspect of embracing a new beginning is to set goals and take action towards achieving them. This can involve pursuing new interests and hobbies, taking on new challenges at work or in our personal lives, or setting goals for personal growth and development. By taking steps towards a new future, we can begin to build momentum and create positive momentum in our lives.

Finally, it is important to cultivate gratitude and appreciation for the present moment. This can involve practicing mindfulness, focusing on the things we are grateful for, and cherishing the relationships and experiences that bring us joy and fulfilment.

Embracing a new beginning after heartbreak is a process that takes time and effort. It requires us to be patient, kind, and compassionate with ourselves, and to be willing to take risks and try new things. By focusing on self-love, setting goals, and cultivating gratitude, we can create a bright and fulfilling future for ourselves, filled with joy, purpose, and meaning.

One important strategy is to practice forgiveness. This can involve forgiving ourselves for any mistakes we may have made in the past, as well as forgiving others who may have hurt us. Forgiveness is not about condoning or excusing harmful behaviour, but rather about releasing the negative emotions and resentment that can hold us back from moving forward.

Another important aspect of embracing a new beginning is to focus on our personal values and beliefs. This means identifying the things that are most important to us in life, and aligning our goals and actions with those values. By living in accordance with our values, we can create a sense of purpose and meaning in our lives, and feel more fulfilled and content.

It is also important to stay open to new experiences and opportunities. This may involve taking risks and stepping outside of our comfort zones, but it can also lead to exciting new possibilities and growth. By staying open and curious, we can discover new passions and interests, and create a life that is full of excitement and adventure.

Finally, it is important to remember that embracing a new beginning is not about forgetting or erasing the past. It is about acknowledging the pain and hurt we have experienced, and using that experience as a catalyst for growth and transformation. By embracing our past, we can create a future that is even brighter and more fulfilling than we ever imagined.

In conclusion, embracing a new beginning after heartbreak requires us to be patient, kind, and compassionate with ourselves. It involves practicing self-love, forgiveness, and gratitude, and aligning our goals and actions with our personal values and beliefs. By staying open to new experiences and embracing our past, we can create a life that is full of joy, purpose, and meaning.

103

"Finding beauty in the imperfection of life and accepting that everything is constantly changing"

~Sanket chaudhary